Exodus and Exile

EXODUS AND EXILE

*The Structure of the
Jewish Holidays*

MONFORD HARRIS

FORTRESS PRESS   MINNEAPOLIS

EXODUS AND EXILE
The Structure of the Jewish Holidays

Scripture quotations unless otherwise noted are from *The TANAKH: The New JPS Translation According to the Traditional Hebrew Text*. Copyright © 1985 by the Jewish Publication Society. Used by permission.

"Christmas and Hanukkah: Two Structurings of the World," by Monford Harris, originally appeared in *Jewish Frontier*, Vol. 43, No. 10, December 1976, pp. 19-21. Reprinted by permission.

"The Jewish Prayer for Rain," by Monford Harris, originally appeared in *Conservative Judaism*, Vol. 37, No. 4, Summer 1984, pp. 79-82. Reprinted by permission.

"Passover: The Seder as Entree into History," by Monford Harris, originally appeared in *JUDAISM*, Vol. 25, No. 2, Spring 1976. Reprinted by permission.

"Purim: The Celebration of Disorder," by Monford Harris, originally appeared in *JUDAISM*, Vol. 26, No. 2, Spring 1977. Reprinted by permission.

Interior design: Judy Gilats, Peregrine Publications
Cover design: Patricia Boman
Cover photo: Corni Shofar. Praga, Museo del Vecchio Cim. Ebraico.

Library of Congress Cataloging-in-Publication Data

Harris, Monford, 1920–
    Exodus and exile : the structure of the Jewish holidays / Monford Harris.
        p.   cm.
    Includes bibliographical references and index.
    ISBN 0-8006-2651-6 (alk. paper)
    1. Fasts and feasts—Judaism—History. I. Title.
BM690.H26   1992
296.4'3—dc20   91-44014
                                                                   CIP

The paper used in this publication meets the minimum requirements of American National Standard for Information Sciences—Permanence of Paper for Printed Library Materials, ANSI Z329.48-1984.   ∞ ™

Manufactured in the U.S.A.   AF 1-2651

96   95   94   93   92   1   2   3   4   5   6   7   8   9   10

To
Moshe Harris Z' 'L
My Grandfather
who taught me
Torah
and to
My Grandchildren
who will continue
the Tradition

Contents

Preface

This book is a study of the presuppositions and gestalt of the Jewish holidays. Neither hortatory nor simply descriptive, it is interpretive.

Thus, this book is neither an attempt at a new code of Jewish law nor a new Jewish catalog. It is also not an analysis of all the details of Jewish practices. Many important Jewish pieties, practices, and customs are not so much as mentioned in this book.

I am most grateful to Dr. Rivkah Harris, my wife, for her encouragement, advice, and close reading of the manuscript.

I wish to thank the Cohn Scholars Fund of Spertus College for its generous grant, which was of great help.

And I am indebted to Ms. Sandra Ballard for typing this study. Both her talent and her graciousness were invaluable.

The Passover chapter has been published in part in *JUDAISM*, Vol. 25, No. 2, Spring 1976; the Purim chapter has been published in *JUDAISM*, Vol. 26, No. 2, Spring 1977; the Hanukkah chapter has been published in part in the *Jewish Frontier*, December 1976; the Geshem Prayer has been published in *Conservative Judaism*, Vol. 37, No. 4, Summer 1984. For the most part, the transliterations of the *Encyclopaedia Judaica* have been followed.

Exodus and Exile

INTRODUCTION

TIME AND HISTORY IN JEWISH EXISTENCE

JEWISH FESTIVALS ARE pivotal points in the Jewish year, embodying Jewish covenantal concerns and motifs and a covenantal sense of time. Jewish existence has shaped many aspects of these festivals; and, in turn, these festivals have informed and shaped Jewish existence. Just as, according to Ahad ha-Am, Sabbath guarded the Jews at times even more than the Jews guarded the Sabbath, so too, the holidays organized and shaped Jewish existence more than the Jews influenced and structured the holidays.

These holidays embody a sense of time and historical reality. One of the central themes in Jewish existence is the Exodus from Egypt. The Exodus is the motif of the three pilgrimage festivals, and it permeates the liturgy of the other holidays, of the Sabbath, and of the daily prayers.

1

THE INTENTION TO GO TO ANOTHER PLACE

Jewish existence has always been characterized by a sense of time and history. Unlike many peoples whose consciousness is (or has been) ahistorical and whose pieties and festivals are structured along lines of fertility and reproduction, Jewish existence and, therefore, its celebrations have always been historically oriented.

How did Jewish existence develop this historical sense in the ancient Near East? Scripture has the ancient Israelite farmer reciting a unique prayer: "A wandering Aramean was my father and he went down into Egypt, and he sojourned there, few in number and he became there a nation . . . And the Egyptians dealt ill with us . . . And we cried unto the Lord . . . And the Lord brought us forth out of Egypt with a mighty hand . . . And he hath brought us unto this place . . . a land flowing with milk and honey."[1] Unique in that it deals with fertility through the framework of historical events, this prayer is but one example of the singular quality of Jewish piety. Modern scholarship has been aware of this historical orientation of Judaism. It has devoted a great deal of attention to the pilgrimage festivals referred to in scripture. Bypassing the traditional claim that these festivals were ordained by God, modern scholarship has analyzed them as having been originally pastoral and agricultural festivals reinterpreted and reworked so that they became celebrations of historic events. Scholars have pondered the question as to how this happened. Nowhere else in the ancient Near East or in the European arena did such an achievement take place.

If, for the sake of discussion, we proceed with the basic assumption of modern secular scholarship and bypass the traditional assumption, seeking to understand how it happened that ancient Israel restructured the pastoral, agricultural festivals so that they became celebrations of historic events, we must understand these festivals as being structured by the historical consciousness of ancient Israel. But how did this historical consciousness—the memory of historic events in the past, an awareness of the past's impact on the present, and a sense of the future, a consciousness different in kind from what has been called the archaic consciousness of both primitive and high cultures—occur in ancient Israel? This historical consciousness must have been deeply rooted in the life situation of the Israelites. It did not come about by intellectual fiat or by contemplating alternatives to the archaic mentality.

THE CALL TO GO

Yi-fu Tuan in his book *Space and Place* suggests that the "intention to go to a place creates historical time: the place is a goal in the future."[2] The intention to go to a place, a goal in the future, is the dynamic of Jewish existence. The act of faithfulness and personal piety that initiates Jewish existence and its historical consciousness is Abraham's response to God's call to leave his native land and go to another land, a place he will be shown. The young Isaac joins his father in responding to God's call to go to the land of Moriah. In turn, Jacob, who was born and, it would seem, settled in the Land, carries out an imposed intention to go to another land in order to escape his brother's wrath. And during all those years working for Laban, he intends to go back to the other place at some future time. In the course of carrying out his intention to return to and settle down in the Land, Jacob instead goes down to Egypt because of all that has happened, although he intends to return to the Land in the future. Indeed, he is promised by God that he will be "brought up" to the Land once again. On arrival in Egypt Joseph's brothers tell the Pharaoh that they have come only to sojourn (Gen. 47:4). Implied is the intention to return to their former place, although "now" they dwell in Goshen. At his death Jacob instructs Joseph about his burial in the Land, just as at his death Joseph instructs his brothers.

In subtle ways scripture depicts the Israelites as intending to go to the Land in the future. Even the new Pharaoh who did not know Joseph did know of the Israelites' intention to go to their own land, and therefore enslaved them (Exod. 1:9-11).

When he is commissioned at Sinai as Exodus leader, Moses is told that Pharaoh's heart will be hardened so that he will not readily let the Israelites go, and that there will be a series of plagues. Although not mentioned in the text, one of the results of the hardening of the Pharaoh's heart was the strengthening of Israel's intention to go, or at least of Moses' intention. Moses had to achieve this. We note this in the account of Moses naming his firstborn son Gershom because "I have been a stranger [*ger*] in a strange land" (Exod. 2:22). Moses understands himself as an Egyptian in Midian; Egypt was the land of his nativity, and an Egyptian he appeared to be in the eyes of Jethro's daughters.

The intention to go to a place that is a goal in the future is not easily sustained. The Joseph generation, the brothers and their families who entered Egypt, did not intend to settle in Egypt. But their descendants were born in Egypt; it was their native land. Yet they must have embodied a determination to go to that other place; for they did not, in the course of time, "go native." When Moses returned to Egypt and told the Israelites of God's message, "the people believed" (Exod. 4:31). What saved them from going native was the intention to go to that other land.

THE NONCIRCULAR EXODUS

Modern scholarship has raised some fundamental and stimulating questions about the nature and composition of the Pentateuch. It judges the Pentateuch to be a product of a time much later than the Mosaic era, a compilation of various traditions embodying different perspectives that were redacted and put together much later in the Land of Israel. These conclusions, about which critical questions can be raised, do not vitiate our analysis; in a sense they reinforce what we maintain. For, if the Pentateuch was composed in the Land of Israel some time after the Israelites had settled there, then it is a most unusual work, because it purports to have been composed outside the Land. Its underlying assumption from the perspective of time is the future, when the Israelites "will come" to the Land. The Pentateuch presupposes an intention toward the future. It is not surprising therefore that three pilgrimage festivals celebrate the Exodus from Egypt while no holiday celebrates the entrance or conquest of the Land.

The Pentateuch—never referring to the Land as the "Land of Israel," for the Israelites have not as yet entered it—embodies, as we have said, an intention to go to the Land in the future. It is oriented both implicitly and explicitly toward the Land as a goal in the future. The great poignancy of the Torah is that Moses (and the entire generation of the Exodus, aside from two exceptions) does not enter the Land. And the great poignancy of Jewish existence has been Exile, not achieving the goal of living in the Land.

The intention to go to the Land of Israel created and maintained a sense of historical time for Jewish existence, and it gave rise to basic categories of Jewish thought and vocabulary. James Muilenberg, reflecting on the Hebrew terms for *way* and *road*, wrote, "This symbol was an expression of the onward movement of time within her [i.e., Israel's] life, its historical character, its ever-changing vicissitudes . . . The road was a peculiarly congenial symbol since it had figured so largely in the epochal movements of Israel's life."[3] Professor Muilenberg adds the important statement, "This road was not a circular turning"[4]; for the circular turning would be the metaphor for the archaic, ahistorical myth of the eternal return.

EXODUS AND EXILE IN JEWISH EXISTENCE

The Exodus, that very early intention to go to that place which was a goal in the future, a central biblical and postbiblical theme of Jewish existence, is counterbalanced by another reality in Jewish historic existence: Exile. Exile means that Jewish existence is once again outside of the Land, that Jewish existence has the intention to go to the Land that is its goal in the future. Exodus and Exile are the polarities of Jewish existence. The daily prayers, the holiday prayers, the holidays themselves—indeed, the entire Jewish tradition—embody and constantly express not only the Exodus event but also the reality of Exile.

EXILE IN JEWISH OBSERVANCES

The observances that most explicitly express the reality of Exile are the Passover Seder, the fast of the Ninth of Av, and the Purim celebration.

The Passover Seder that celebrates the Exodus from slavery unto freedom makes its participants fully sensitive to their situation in Exile. The very first paragraph of the Seder's liturgy states it: "Now we are here, next year [may we be] in the Land

of Israel; now we are slaves; next year [may we be] free men."
Declarations such as "In every generation they rise against us
to destroy us" and the Seder's conclusion, "Next year in Jerusalem," assert the reality of Exile.

The fast of the Ninth of Av is obviously an expression of the
reality of Exile. It deals with Exile as contradiction of Exodus.
Some of the liturgical poems express this explicitly. The Ninth
of Av is a day of fasting and weeping; it is a concentrated suffering
of Exile.

Purim also deals with Exile, so it is preceded by a fast; but
Purim laughs at Exile, seeing it as incongruity rather than as
contradiction of Exodus. It deals with Exile as comedy.

The three pilgrimage festivals whose focal point is Exodus are
conscious of Exile; the morning additional service declares, "Because of our sins we have been exiled from our Land . . ." Of
the three festivals, Passover, *the* celebration of Exodus, makes
the strongest statement about Exile because its banquet of a free
people has been celebrated for two thousand years in the exilic
situation.

The high holy days also refer to Exile. Rosh Ha-Shanah with
its themes of repentance and God's judgment presupposes repentance within the context of Exile. The prayer *U-Netanneh Tokef*
recited on the high holy days, written by Kalonymus ben Me-
shullam Kalonymus in the eleventh century, is traditionally
known as The Prayer of Amnon of Mainz, a tenth-century martyr
whose limbs were amputated, because he did not seriously consider conversion to Christianity, by the Bishop of Mainz. This
legend, current even in our time, is one of the exilic themes of
these Days of Awe.

The Day of Atonement makes the Jew acutely aware of the
existential reality of Exile. The martyrdom of the ten holy sages—
pictured as taking place in the Land conquered by the Romans—
is recited on this day and gives the congregation an awareness
of its situation in Exile. The day's liturgical theme of the sacrifices
in the Temple, with a detailed description of the high priest's
performing these sacrifices, and the expressed sorrow that these
channels of pardon are no longer available, points to the exilic
awareness of that other place, the Land of Israel. The proclamation at the end of the closing service, "Next Year in Jerusalem,"
also expresses the day's sense of Exile.

Even the Sabbath with its themes of creation, Exodus, and the Time-World-to-Come makes one aware of the reality of Exile. Solomon Alkabetz's Sabbath hymn *L'cha Dodi*, composed in Safed, refers in a number of stanzas to the exilic situation. The *Av ha-Rahmim* prayer, recited on most Sabbaths, an elegy composed perhaps during the First Crusade over the martyred Jewish communities, also imparts a sense of Exile.

ON THE ROAD TO A FUTURE GOAL

As the theme of Exodus with its intention to go to another place in the future shaped Jewish historical consciousness, so, too, Exile shaped and maintained Jewish historical consciousness.

These polarities are unique to Jewish existence. It is worth noting that the great classic work *Hasting's Encyclopedia of Religion and Ethics* has no articles on Exodus or Exile. *The New Catholic Encyclopedia* has an article on Exodus and one on Diaspora, each dealing only with biblical material. Exodus and Exile are uniquely Jewish realities. The Exodus/Exile themes presuppose the Jewish people on the road to a goal in the future.

Exodus is a basic and consistent theme in Jewish piety for a number of reasons. God's sovereignty must be affirmed by the Jewish people not because He created the universe, for in that case all human beings owe Him fealty; but the Jews must accept His kingship since He freed them from slavery and thereby became their Lord. Secondly, only one generation actually experienced the Exodus. Much must be done and said, therefore, so that in every generation every Jew will see himself or herself *as if* having gone out of Egypt; for how can every subsequent generation know existentially that which it did not directly experience? Thirdly, the Exodus from Egypt has been eclipsed during the last two thousand years by Exile. This Exile of such long duration and profound despair might obliterate from Jewish existence the awareness of Exodus. What meaning can Exodus have for those in the devastating situation of Exile? How can one square Exodus with Exile? These are the reasons why the memory of Exodus must be stressed.

Should Exodus be forgotten, there would be no intention to go to that other place, the Land, the goal in the future. Should Exodus be forgotten, the historical consciousness of the Jewish people would no longer exist. Jews would "go native" wherever they were. There would no longer be Exile. The Jews would be submerged in the autochthonous population of the various lands they inhabit.

Jewish existence, however, has managed to live the paradox of Exodus-Exile. The days of the week point to the Sabbath, which is an embodiment of Exodus and Redemption lived in Exile, as are the holidays. The Jewish people's outstanding characteristic is its great historical consciousness. The holidays have both shaped that consciousness and are the very diurnal living of that consciousness.

Chapter 1

SABBATH

COVENANTAL TIME

ONLY THE JEWS regularly celebrate the creation of the world by observing the Sabbath. The celebration, according to the tradition, is incumbent only on the Jew.

Not all Jews faithfully observed the Sabbath early in their history. There were Sabbath violators in the desert: the stick-gatherer and the would-be manna-gatherers.[1] In the Land of Israel, too, scripture indicates, the community as a whole was not devoutly Sabbath-observant. In the postbiblical period the Jews observed the Sabbath, even raising the question of the propriety of self-defense on the Sabbath. During the last two thousand years, except for the modern emancipation era, the community as a whole observed the Sabbath.

Sabbath has been celebrated for the most part in Exile because much of Jewish existence has been spent in Exile. Significantly, the first reference to a group of Jews observing the Sabbath is to a group outside the Land, the tribe of Levi in pre-Exodus Egypt. And Moses—the most poignant exilic Jew, for God Himself denied Moses entree into the Land—is particularly associated with the Sabbath. Moses, says the tradition, asked Pharaoh to grant the Israelites a seventh-day rest.[2] And it was Moses who was informed by God that He had a gift for the people: the Sabbath.[3] The Sabbath morning Amidah refers to Moses' joy at "giving his portion," i.e., the Sabbath. Yet Moses, never having entered the Land, was an exilic Israelite.

In many ways Sabbath is associated with Exile. The rabbinic statement, "If Israel were to keep two Sabbaths according to the laws thereof they would be redeemed immediately,"[4] expresses the exilic ambience of Sabbath. The joyous Sabbath liturgical composition, *L'cha Dodi*, composed in the Land, refers to Exile in five of its nine stanzas.

A TIME OF COVENANTAL INTIMACY

One tradition states that all the commandments were given publicly except the Sabbath commandment, which was given in secret.[5] Thus the Sabbath was given in a situation of intimacy. The proof text cited by the sages indicates this: "It is a sign between Me and the Children of Israel forever" (Exod. 31:17).

GOD'S GIFT TO ISRAEL

Sabbath is the time of covenantal intimacy. That is why Sabbath is God's *gift* to Israel. A gift is "An outcome and strengthening of the covenant . . . a necessary result of a real relationship between individuals . . . [which the gift] creates or strengthens."[6] Sabbath as gift strengthens the covenantal relationship between God and the Jews. Sabbath, therefore, is particularly associated with Exile. It is during the long Exile that the covenant had to be strengthened and confirmed. Exile can weaken Israel's sense of the covenant, for Exile can corrode the faithfulness of the community. In a deeper sense than secularly oriented Ahad ha-Am realized, Sabbath guarded the Jews; for Sabbath strengthened Jewish covenantal faithfulness.

THE ACTIVITY OF REST

Sabbath brings rest to the community, a rest created by God on the seventh day, according to the tradition.[7] Sabbath rest is a kind of activity. The role of the senses on the Sabbath indicates this. Sabbath observance calls all the senses into play. The optic sense is stimulated by the Sabbath candles. The auditory sense is active in the recitation of kiddush, table songs, Torah reading, prayers, and study. Sabbath eve is the time for sexual intercourse, in which the tactile sense is crucial. Both the gustatory and olfactory senses are active in the Sabbath emphasis on food. The rabbinic references to preparation for the Sabbath stress food. Shammai and Hillel, who differ in regard to other Sabbath preparations, agree on the subject of food purchases. Traditional Jewish sources inevitably stress Sabbath food. Certain foods are deemed preferable. Even the number of meals to be eaten on the Sabbath is discussed. It is considered meritorious to eat warm food; one medieval sage suspected the rejection of warm food to be a mark of heresy.[8] Fasting, other than on a Yom Kippur Sabbath, is forbidden. Roman emperors, the Talmud tells us, were aware of the fragrance of Sabbath food. Seeking an explanation of its source, they were told that the aroma was that of a spice called *Sabbath*.[9]

While all the senses operate on the Sabbath, touch, taste, and smell have especially prominent roles. W. H. Hudson, the British writer and naturalist, has suggested that "smell . . . may be classed with taste . . . Smell is in fact 'taste at a distance.' "[10] And there is something tactile about taste. Unlike seeing and hearing, the distance-covering senses, touch, taste, and smell are the "intimate senses" because they are involved with the organic life processes.[11] In contrast to the optic and auditory senses, which are the "defining senses," the intimate senses "are the direct, important sources of meaning, of worth, of value."[12] Smell, in particular, has been ignored and implicitly devalued in Western culture. Yet Hudson considered it to be "more emotional . . . and [it] stirs the mind more deeply than seeing or hearing."[13] Hudson reports that the English poet laureate William Wordsworth lacked the olfactory sense but in his garden one day suddenly smelled the fragrance of the flowers and described it as being like "a vision of Paradise."[14] This, we suggest, is why fragrance is important on the Sabbath.

Touch, the most realistic of the senses,[15] is also the most intimate. Touch, the sense most devalued by Maimonides, was defended by the medieval *Epistle on Holiness* (Iggeret Ha-Kodesh), the concern of which is sexual intercourse on Sabbath eve.

THE INTIMACY OF WISDOM

It has been suggested that a certain type of wisdom can be communicated by the three intimate senses, which have "a language and wisdom of their own . . . The language of intimate sense wisdom is symbolism that can hint and suggest meanings that are indescribable [but that give] trust, confidence, faith, and hope."[16] This is what the senses communicate on the Sabbath, the day that strengthens Jewish trust, confidence, faithfulness, and hope in God.

In the middle ages the custom arose of reciting Song of Songs, the most sensuous text in Jewish traditional literature, shortly before welcoming the Sabbath. Its recitation prepares one for Sabbath by stimulating all the senses. Sabbath is necessarily the most sensuous time, since it celebrates the creation of this sensuous world, and it is the senses that appropriate the world. According to an old tradition, on the eve of the Sabbath God gives each Jew a *neshamah yeterah*, not an oversoul as moderns interpret it, but, as Rashi explains, "a greater amplitude or openness for enjoying food and drink."[17] The recitation of Song of Songs readies one for receiving the *neshamah yeterah*.

Reciting Song of Songs is also an act of preparation for the Sabbath because it is the classical Jewish statement of intimacy; and Sabbath, the one commandment given intimately as covenantal gift, is the time for intimate relationship.

Sabbath intimacy is expressed in many ways. A recurrent Sabbath theme is that of Bride and Groom. According to the midrash, Sabbath complained to God that as the last day of the week she lacked a mate; God answered that the community of Israel is Sabbath's mate.[18] The welcoming-Sabbath hymn *L'cha Dodi*, using the theme of lovers, refers to the joy of bride and groom; indeed, the first words of the hymn are from Song of Songs. Another aspect of Sabbath as intimate, covenantal time is the tradition that Friday night is the time for sexual intercourse. This human intimacy is rooted in the covenantal intimacy between God and Israel. Song of Songs is, therefore, a song of man-woman love and, at the same time, a song of love between God and the Jewish community.

Modern scholarship understands Song of Songs as a late compilation of erotic poetry. It judges the traditional Jewish interpretation that the song is about God and Israel to be a superimposed, artificial interpretation, which it obliquely dismisses. Chaim Rabin, in his study "The Song of Songs and Tamil Poetry,"[19] argues, however, that the so-called late-linguistic forms and vocabulary "place [it] squarely in the First Temple period . . . in the heyday of Judean trade with South Arabia and beyond (and this may include the lifetime of King Solomon) by someone who had travelled to South Arabia and South India . . . had there become acquainted with Tamil poetry [and] . . . took over its recurrent themes and certain stylistic features. . ."[20]

It is possible, Professor Rabin speculates, that Song of Songs was written "as an allegory for the pining of the people of Israel or perhaps the human soul for God . . . [and] the erotic longing of the maiden as a simile for the need of man for God."[21] Referring to a medieval Tamil legend of a girl who loved a god, Rabin says, "Thus the use of the genre of love poetry of this kind for the expression of religious longing may have been borrowed from India."[22]

Song of Songs, initially or subsequently both biography and metaphor, is fittingly recited at the ushering in of Sabbath, for it is the classical Jewish statement of intimacy in the human realm and in the Divine-Israel encounter.

Ahavah, the only word for *love* in Song of Songs, occurs there some seventeen times. While it has been fashionable in certain gentile circles to distinguish between agape and eros, to the derogation of the latter, Song of Songs does not embody this distinction. *Ahavah* is used for loving neighbor, for loving God, and for God's loving Israel.[23] Love, however, "is not a more or less superficial sentiment. It is identical with peace [shalom] itself, with the unity of the wills."[24]

Shalom is important in the Sabbath vocabulary. Psalm 29, recited at the welcoming of Sabbath, concludes with this word. The Sabbath evening service contains the phrases "Tabernacle of Shalom" and "Lord of Shalom." The Song of the Angels sung on returning home from the synagogue contains *shalom* in each stanza. *Shabbat Shalom* is a traditional Sabbath greeting. Love and peace constitute the Sabbath.

PROHIBITIONS

It has long been noted that Sabbath is richer in prohibitions than in positive acts. The prohibitions and subprohibitions—e.g., *mukzeh*, what must not be handled, Sabbath domains and boundaries—fill the rabbinic texts, commentaries, codes, and responses. Millions of words have been written on the subject of Sabbath prohibitions. The prohibitions are massive and detailed, broad and minute.

Prohibitions are intrinsic to the Sabbath. There is good reason for this structure of prohibitions. First, Sabbath must always be guarded. To observe the Sabbath means to guard the Sabbath from profanation. For Sabbath, not rooted in the cycles of nature, is fragile and depends on a small, fragmented, and scattered people. Sabbath's nature necessitates prohibitions, "fences" that protect it from profanation.

But there is another reason for Sabbath prohibitions. Kenneth Burke, the literary critic, has noted that "there are no negations in nature; any natural condition being what it is."[25] In other words, there are no "shalt-nots," no prohibitions in the natural sphere. *Thou Shalt Not* comes from the sphere of the personal, human or divine. Sabbath is not a natural reality. The Sabbath day is different from other days; it is blessed by God. The prohibitions are aspects of the personal.

THE SOCIAL REALITY OF FIRE

One of the oldest Sabbath prohibitions is the kindling of fire. Two kinds of fire occur in reality: naturally initiated fire and fire ignited by humans. In the natural dimension things burn. But humans make fire, an artifact of immense cultural significance.

In his *The Psychoanalysis of Fire*, the philosopher Gaston Bachelard wrote that "fire is more a social reality than a *natural reality*" (his emphasis);[26] and, even though unaware of the primary prohibition of the Sabbath, he nonetheless asserted that "the social prohibitions are the first."[27]

It is not accidental that, while the Pentateuch prohibits work on the Sabbath, the one specific prohibition it mentions is kindling a fire. We suggest that this is because fire is man's most effective tool for manipulating the world. O. C. Stewart, in his study "Fire as the First Great Force Employed by Man," concluded that "fire has been used by man to influence his geographic environment during his entire career as a human."[28] Fire kindling is prohibited on the Sabbath because the Jew must not manipulate the world on the Sabbath.

AT PEACE WITH CREATION

According to Erich Fromm, "Sabbath is a day of peace between man and nature; work of any kind is a disturbance of the man-nature equilibrium. By not working man is free from the chains of time, although for only one day a week."[29] He explains the significance of this work stoppage: "Stopping interference with nature for one day you eliminate time; where there is no change, no work, no human interference there is no time."[30]

Nowhere in the biblical-rabbinic tradition, the tradition that structures the Sabbath, is there a notion of eliminating time. Time and creation (Fromm's "nature") are not considered to be burdens (Fromm's "chains"). Fromm's interpretation of the Sabbath is a strange mixture of a gnostic devaluation of the natural world and of a high value attached to "man-nature equilibrium." Furthermore, his idea of freedom "from the chains of time" platonizes the Sabbath and misses something vital, because "the security of a normal human being does not lie in liberation from time. Temporal pressure is constricting but it is also the framework with which our personality is organized."[31] *Sabbath is intimate time.* Work is prohibited because the world and its creatures are not to be manipulated.

The primal document on the Sabbath is scripture. The tradition structures the Sabbath for Jewish existence, embodying scriptural premises. Unlike our mechanistic world picture, scripture "does not distinguish between a living and lifeless nature . . . The earth is a living thing . . . with which man must make himself familiar when he wants to use it; he must respect . . . and not do violence to it while appropriating it . . . Even the plants and trees have a life which is to be absorbed and exploited but not violated . . . [T]he relation between the earth and its owner . . . is a covenant relation . . . and the owner does not solely prevail in the relation . . . [He must] uphold its blessing and take what it yields on its own accord."[32] This is true of fauna also. "Man has a covenant with his cattle . . . he must not weaken the lives of the cattle. Cattle and servants shall be permitted to rest every seventh day."[33] Johannes Pedersen, the biblical scholar whose words we have been quoting, explains this covenant with the animals, which could also be applied to flora and plots of land, as "the covenant with the beasts means an intimacy."[34]

No work is done on the Sabbath, for work is nothing other than the manipulation of creatures and creation. Manipulation would violate intimacy.

EACH DEPENDING ON THE OTHER

Thinkers are only now beginning to attend to the question of intimacy. Much thought has been given to the problem of anomie or alienation, but intimacy has received very little attention.[35] Georg Simmel, however, did deal with the subject of intimacy. Simmel pointed out that "the basis of intimacy is personal inter-dependence and does not result in a structure that goes beyond its elements."[36] By this he means that "the intimate character of certain relations . . . derive[s] from the individual's inclination to consider that which distinguishes him from others, that which is individual in a qualitative sense, as the core, value, and chief matter of his existence."[37] Intimacy is not necessarily sexual; for, as Simmel explained, "intimacy is not based on the *content* of the relationship . . . Only that is intimate which . . . [the individual exclusive] functions as the vehicle or axis of the relationship itself."[38]

Intimacy does not necessarily presuppose only two individuals. Intimacy "can be noted in regard to groups. They, too, make their specific content, that is shared only by the members, not by outsiders, their centers and real fulfillments . . ."³⁹

Sabbath is intimate time between God and the covenantal community. From this the other intimacies derive. Sabbath is, therefore, time for the great human intimacy of sexual intercourse, for intimacy "is based on what each of the two participants gives or shows only to one other person and to nobody else."⁴⁰

Simmel's phrase "the intimacy of the dyad" refers to what Jews would call covenantal intimacy. In reflecting on the intimacy of the dyad, Simmel concluded, "Precisely the fact that each of the two knows that he can depend only upon the other and on nobody else, gives the dyad a special consecration."⁴¹ This gives the dyadic covenantal intimacy of the Sabbath its special consecration: both God and Israel know that each can depend only on the other. During the whole course of Jewish existence both have recognized their interdependence in the matter of the weekly celebration of creation. God depends on Israel to observe the Sabbath as Israel depends on God to grant the Sabbath, its peace and love and the Sabbath rest, which is also His creation.

The tradition understandably declares that a Gentile must not observe the Sabbath. "Everyday experiences," Simmel makes us realize, "show the specific character that a relationship attains by the fact that only two elements participate in it. A common fate or enterprise, an agreement or secret between two persons, ties each of them in a very different manner than if only three have a part in it."⁴² Rationalist Jewish thinkers, including some rationalist halakists, have argued that Sabbath observance testifies to the noneternity of the world. For these thinkers Sabbath observance is nothing other than a metaphysical statement. It should follow, therefore, that all people ought to observe the Sabbath. Yet the halakah would forbid this. Rightly so; Sabbath is intimate, covenantal time into which a third party is not invited.

A classical Sabbath text is the medieval *Raza de Shabbat*,⁴³ often understood as the *Secret of Sabbath*. But *raz* means more than "secret"; it is the equivalent of the Hebrew *sod*, which means "intimate union."⁴⁴ *Raza de Shabbat* proclaims Sabbath as "Intimate Time." In this sense, Sabbath relates to the creation of the world. The Jew observing the Sabbath does not manipulate the world. He appropriates it covenantly.

Chapter 2

PASSOVER

THE SEDER AS ENTREE INTO HISTORY

PASSOVER IS THE ONLY festival that has three variations: *Pesach Mizraim*, the first Passover celebrated in Egypt; *Pesach Dorot*, the Passover celebrated throughout the generations; *Pesach Sheni*, observed only during Temple times by those unable to celebrate the regular Passover.

NEITHER A PARADIGM NOR A NOSTALGIC ACT

The Egyptian Passover was celebrated only once, when the Children of Israel left Egypt. According to the rabbinic sources the Egyptian Passover was unique: only then did the Jews eat in haste, loins girded, shoes on feet, staff in hand, following the biblical rules. There was, however, no Seder—no recitation, no questions and answers, no dipping, no reclining. No one proclaimed, "Next year in Jerusalem." Presumably, no one then had heard of Jerusalem.

That the Egyptian Passover was celebrated only once is significant. The last supper of the Jews in Egypt, some thirty-five hundred years ago, was not the paradigm for the Seder of the generations.

Paradigms are found in traditional and archaic societies that "make every effort to disregard"[1] history. Such societies are characterized by a "revolt against concrete historical time . . . a nostalgia for a periodical return to the mythical time of the beginning of things."[2] Furthermore, "in the particulars of his conscious behavior . . . the archaic man acknowledges no act which has not been previously posited and lived by someone else, some other being who was not a man. What he does has been done before. His life is the ceaseless repetition of gestures initiated by others."[3] The Seder is not an act of nostalgia for a return to mythical time at the beginning of things. It does not embody the ceaseless repetition of gestures initiated by others. Indeed, there were long periods of time when Passover was not observed.

It is recorded that Hezekiah, king of Judah (seventh–eighth centuries B.C.E.), urged everyone, including the northern Israelites, to observe *Pesach Sheni* because the regular Passover had not been observed. In letters he sent throughout the land he admonished the people to return to God so that God "may return to the remnant that are escaped of you out of the hands of the kings of Assyria; and be not like your fathers and like your brethren, who acted treacherously against the Lord . . . Now be ye not stiffnecked as your fathers were."[4] Hezekiah's criticism of the ancestors and his reference to a historic event, the conquest by the Assyrian kings, indicate that Passover was not ceaseless repetition of a primal gesture in order to escape history.

Noteworthy, too, is the account of Josiah's reformation. In 621 B.C.E. the discovery of a scroll in the Temple chest led the king to reinstitute the observance of the Passover; "there was not kept such a Passover from the days of the judges that judged Israel, nor in all the days of the kings of Israel, nor of the kings of Judah; but in the eighteenth year of the king Josiah was this Passover kept to the Lord in Jerusalem."[5]

The nature of "such a Passover" is not recorded, but the statement about the long period of time during which it was *not* celebrated, perhaps as much as six hundred years, is significant.

The account embodies a sense of history and an implicit criticism of the ancestors.

LANGUAGE OF COMMUNITY ORDER

The Seder is central to the Passover of the generations, and Recitation is central to the Seder. Even the foods presuppose recitation. In a sense the function of the Seder is to elicit recitation. Many of the specific acts of the Seder are done so as to evoke questions from the children, with adult recitation in response. The goal of the Seder is to make the generations existentially aware of the Exodus.

The strong possibility was that the Exodus from Egypt would be forgotten. A people does not remember an event that took place in its dim past. Therefore, each generation of children, those who will be the next generation of adults, must be made to remember that which they did not experience. All the succeeding generations are the nonexperiencing progeny of the generation that went out of Egypt.

No questions were asked at the last meal in Egypt. Yet questions are inherent to the holiday of Passover. Passover is the only holiday that Scripture tells the people to explain "when thy son asketh thee in time to come."[6] The Passover Haggadah has many questions, from the well-known four questions to the queries of the rabbis to the song of "Who knows one." Questions are not simply an aspect of the literary style of the Haggadah. A halakist has stated that

> the recounting of the Exodus from Egypt must be done by way of question and answer. Even if a person is alone [i.e., a one-person Seder] he must ask himself "why is this night different" because this is one of the rules of the recounting [of the Exodus], that it be by way of question and answer . . . Basically, the obligation is to respond on the matter of the Exodus of Egypt to one who asks . . . For this is the way of question and answer: another asks and he [the questioned one] answers. There must, therefore, be another who asks.[7]

BECOMING AWARE OF A CREATED ORDER

Questions are so intrinsic to the Seder that the opening statement, "This is the bread of affliction," was interpreted by a rabbinic sage to mean the bread "to which we *respond* with many words."[8] The first of the responses is the four questions, asked by the youngest child. Should there be no children present, an adult asks. These and the other questions in the Haggadah must be asked.

The phenomenon of questioning has been studied by Erwin Straus, who states,

> It is a questioning being that faces the world when man looks at things, turns to his fellow man or reflects upon himself. The questioner and the person questioned direct themselves, in their question and answer, toward the order of things. The order is understood by each one as one and the same for all of them and, therefore, valid and obligating, tying and binding . . . They understand each other through the order in that they communicate with each other about it.[9]

Prime examples of questioner and answerer are the mother and the child.

> With the question "What is that" the child gives us to understand that he has discovered the universality of language at the same time as *universalia in rebus*. He does not ask his Mother, "What do you call this?" but rather "What is this?" Things are their names, which, after all, appear as imminent attributes of things to the child, all belong to a general order. The child's parents did not create the order. They are familiar with it and know it, but—and this is just what the child's question proves—they are also subject to it. The order, arrived at through the name, is universally valid and universally obligatory.[10]

This is true of the Passover Seder: the child becomes aware of the fact that there is a Seder, an order, that the parents did not create but to which they are subject. They teach it to him, they mediate it to him. The child also becomes aware that his parents are creatures, not creators, of the order that exists independently of them and that is incumbent on both of them.

The Seder directs both of them. This orientation presupposes communication in it and about it. For the child, the Seder is not involved with wish fulfillment for the individual. The four questions are not the private language of childhood. They are the language of community order.

ADDRESSING THE SELF-EXCLUDED

One is not to assume, however, that the child immediately becomes an adult. As Straus explains: "We do not claim that the child knows this content in all its implications. Nevertheless, we are justified in stating that, in questioning, he requests its determination."[11]

The Haggadah presupposes this; the section of the four sons embodies this, taking into account different types of questioners. Some sons know the content in all its implications; some must be urged to ask; and, of those who know the content, some do not request the determination of the answer. The third and fourth sons fit Straus's description: "With his first question . . . with the slow building of his vocabulary the child attains entry into an area that extends far beyond himself into a sphere of order that permits him to shape his own life but also commits him to doing it."[12] The third and fourth sons can be characterized as the ones who are slow in building up vocabulary.

It is significant that it is a wicked son, not a stupid one, who is counterposed to the others. He is the one who rejects entry into an arena that extends beyond his own horizon of physical existence; he refuses to reach beyond himself into another sphere of order. This distinction merits our attention. It is shocking that the Haggadah presupposes a wicked son. Yet the wicked son is a necessary part of the Haggadah, which is finely attuned to Jewish historic existence and to the initial historic situation. In Egypt, in their enslavement, the Israelites had wicked sons. When Moses saw the two Hebrews fighting, he said to the *rasha*, "Wherefore smitest thou thy fellow?" (Exod. 2:13). Johannes Pedersen interprets this passage as Moses "addressed the sinner; i.e., he who was wrong." He adds that "In the conflict between Yahweh and Pharaoh, the latter declared that he had sinned: 'Yahweh is righteous, and I and my people are the sinners (*ha-reshaim*).' "[13]

Pedersen, in discussing "the righteous" and "the *rasha*," explains that

> in a mutual relation he is the righteous who maintains the duties which the fellowship implies for him; he does what he is bound to do; but when the other one does not do his duty, he will not get what is due to him according to the community . . . The sinful deed is by its very essence a breach of peace. But it does not only mean that one neglects giving another what is due to him; it means that one's soul is diseased. The soul only exists as a link in an organism with which it is intimately interwoven. The breach of peace is a result of a soul misjudging this reality and acting as if it were isolated, something apart."[14]

The wicked son is the one who does not do his fellowship duties. He acts as one apart. He, therefore, will not get what is due him according to the community. The Haggadah states it in primal terms: "He excluded himself from the community (the K'lal); had he been there [Egypt] he would not have been redeemed." In Straus's terms, the wicked son excludes himself from the order, he does not "reach beyond himself."

TRANSMITTING THE INSIGHTS

What do those who enter the order achieve? They enter, individually or in groups, the realm of history. The insights gained through questioning are transmittable; they are possessions bequeathed from one generation to the next.

The goal of the Seder is that its participants enter the realm of history because "in every particular generation a person is obliged to see himself as if he went out of Egypt." The "as if" is crucial, perhaps the most sensitive touchstone in the entire Haggadah. A statement of Straus's, whose rhythm is reminiscent of the Haggadah, will serve to clarify the "as if."

> As a questioner he breaks through the confines set by his senses. In the act of thinking, he reaches through the perspectives to the What, . . . from the fragments to the whole, from confusion to clarity. The pleasure inherent in understanding has its source in the transition from the limitations of sensory experience to the view

of the comprehensive order. Nevertheless, in breaking through the horizons of senses, man . . . is held in his place. He is forced to express the whole through parts, the What through perspective images and the timeless through the time bound . . . The representation of the comprehensive order, therefore, requires both humility and courage: humility and patience, and self denial in striving to understand the order in itself, courage in the attempt to represent the whole with particular means.[15]

This is the problem faced by the Haggadah. The Jew must break through the confines set by his senses; he must see himself going out of Egypt. But the Jew is in his particular generation, in his place. He is not in ancient Egypt, nor above time and place. He is here and now. The Haggadah is not a platonic liturgical text, dealing with realms above time and place. The order is the realm of history. The *as if*, then, is the problematic issue.

The *as if* deals with the question of time. In seeing oneself as if one went out of Egypt, one does not deny the present, one does not attempt to reenact the original Exodus. The Passover of the generations is not the Egyptian Passover.

Jewish existence has shown tendencies to celebrate an Egyptian Passover. Some medieval Karaites would leave their homes and region on the first day of Passover as a reenactment of the Exodus.[16] The Samaritan high priest walks to the area where the paschal lamb is being prepared, his loins girded, feet shod, staff in hand, consciously reenacting the Egyptian Passover.[17] The Jews of the Caucasus region would march around with stick and bundle over their shoulders in order to reenact the Exodus from Egypt.[18] Rabbi Hayim Benveniste, seventeenth-century scholar and codifier, said, "It is my custom to take a staff in hand, to tie my shoes, and to say 'thus shall ye eat it: with your loins girded, your shoes on your feet, and your staff in your hand; and ye shall eat it in haste; it is the Lord's Passover [Exod. 12:11]. Therefore, I [also] have the custom not to remove my belt on Passover eve until after the [eating of the] afikoman."[19] Some Jews in the nineteenth and twentieth centuries in Eastern Europe placed the afikoman in a napkin "as a remembrance of that which was said, 'their kneading troughs being bound up in their clothes'; and there are those that place it on their shoulders as a remembrance of the Exodus from Egypt."[20] These individual tendencies should not surprise us. "Men . . . have a tendency to become archetypal and paradigmatic."[21] These individual acts remained private acts. Judah Ashkenazi, eighteenth-century commentator to the *Shulkan Aruch*, says of Benveniste's custom, "In these regions we do not do these things."[22]

DISCUSSING THE EXODUS EVENT

The rules of the Seder do not embody the Egyptian Passover. With its wine, food, and controlled conversation, the Seder is a kind of Jewish symposium. In the classical symposium various subjects were discussed.[23] The Seder symposium had only one subject, discussed in countless sedarim down the centuries: the Exodus event. While "the heavens declare the glory of God, and the firmament showeth His handiwork," the Jews declare and tell *(m'saper* and *magid;* the two verbs used in Psalm 19 and in the Passover Haggadah) of the Exodus event.

An "event" constitutes a problem. Michel Foucault, noting the paucity of thinking on the subject, says that

> an event is neither substance nor accident, nor quality, nor process; events are not corporeal . . . Yet an event is certainly not immaterial; it takes effect, becomes affect, always on the level of materiality. Events . . . consist in relation to, coexistence with, dispersion of, the cross-checking accumulation and the selection of material elements; it occurs as an effect of, and in, material dispersion . . . The philosophy of event should advance in the direction, . . . paradoxical, of an incorporeal materialism.[24]

This incorporeal matter, the Exodus event, "took effect, became affect, always [for thirty-five hundred years] on the level of materiality."

The Seder as dialogue-symposium deals with this. The dialogue is a "mode of inter-human relation . . . made possible only by a transition from a society immobile in its hierarchy of the moment . . . to a society in which equality of relations [is] made possible and assured potential exchange, fidelity to the past, the engagement of the future, and the reciprocity of points of view."[25]

The Seder dialogue embodies fidelity to the past in its telling of the story of the Exodus. The Seder dialogue embodies the engagement of the future in its concern for the generations and in its "Next year in Jerusalem." The Seder dialogue embodies reciprocity of points of view by the various perspectives of the Haggadah.

The Seder is, in all probability, modeled on the classical Greek and Roman banquet.[26] It is tacitly assumed by moderns that this modeling is due to cultural borrowing and that this is historically interesting but not particularly significant. We, however, consider this of great import. Since the Seder is not an act of nostalgia it rejects the Egyptian Passover. It appropriates the banquet of freemen as a vehicle for the celebration of history. It is through this banquet of freemen that one fulfills the obligation to see oneself *as if* one went out of Egypt.

SEEING ONESELF AS OUT OF EGYPT

That one is obliged to *see* oneself as if one went out of Egypt merits attention. The senses have been a subject on which thinkers have reflected. In Western culture there is a conception of a hierarchy of the senses. In the philosophical tradition, sight has been considered the noblest of the senses. Maimonides, speaking within that tradition, considered touch the ignoble sense. David Cohen, an Israeli thinker, concludes that hearing is the specifically Hebraic sense.[27] The Haggadah's statement that one is obliged to *see* oneself can be best understood if we avoid philosophizing that term. Biblical scholar Johannes Pedersen has clarified the Hebrew word meaning "seeing." "It is characteristic that the word which means to see, *ra'a*, not only means the impression received through the eye but also applies to the hearing, to the touch and upon the whole to the reception of any mental impression: one 'sees' heat, misery, hunger, life, and death."[28]

"Seeing," then, is a comprehensive term for all the senses. To see oneself as if one went out of Egypt is to *sense* oneself as if one went out of Egypt. At the Seder, hearing is important because there is recitation; seeing is important because the symbolic foods are pointed to; and taste is important because food is eaten. Indeed, the members of the Seder are made very conscious of food. Aside from Kiddush and Karpas, which refer to ingestion, the first general statement, "this is the bread of affliction," deals with food to be tasted at the Seder. Although "taste is more narrowly circumscribed [than touch, it] . . . designates shrewdness, presumably because it is a particularly critical sense."[29] The senses, then, enable a person to sense himself totally in the order of history.

DIALOGUE OF LOVER AND BELOVED

There is an old tradition of reciting Song of Songs at the conclusion of the Seder. No reason is given for this. Medieval traditions, however, refer to the recitation of Song of Songs on the Sabbath of the intermediate days of Passover. The reason given is that the verse, "I have compared thee, O my love, to a steed in Pharaoh's chariot" (Song of Songs 1:9), indicates that it "speaks of the Exodus from Egypt . . . and the whole matter speaks of the four redemptions [from the four exiles] for the person who understands."[30] Rooted in history, Song of Songs has traditionally been understood as a dialogue between the Lover and the beloved Children of Israel. That Song of Songs is recited at the conclusion is an aspect of the Seder as a Jewish symposium.

The recitation of text that deals with love brings to mind the most famous symposium, that of Plato, the dialogue whose main topic is love and praise of the god of love. A brilliant analysis of Plato's *Symposium* is offered by Stanley Rosen.[31] According to him, "Dialogues, in general, may be defined as educational games,"[32] an insight that can perhaps be applied to the Seder. But the Seder is a different game from Plato's *Symposium*, because "the *Symposium* . . . is a game having as its principal pedagogic function the teaching of the nature and habits of man's psyche."[33] Professor Rosen clarifies this. The *Symposium* is "an evocation of the past, not an historical past but in a mythical sense."[34] This distinction between historical and mythical is important. "The function of myth," Rosen explains, "is to transcend history in return to origins."[35] Consequently, "Plato's turn to the past is thus a turning away from history,"[36] and "a turning . . . toward the mythical past of Socrates' philosophical existence."[37]

Part of Socrates' mythical past in this platonic dialogue is Diotima, the woman who had instructed a young Socrates about love. Her teaching, as summed up by Professor Rosen, was that "Eros is the desire of what we lack, to the extent that we grasp the eternal we must cease to be erotic."[38]

In contrast, the Seder as symposium is not involved with a mythical past, does not transcend history, and in "grasping the eternal" does not cease to love. Its ultimate statement, the recitation of Song of Songs, is a statement of love in history. Alvin Gouldner, in his *Enter Plato*, says of Plato that "he devalues human love."[39] That the Seder's postscript is a collection of love poems that serves as a metaphor for the covenantal love between God and the Jews is another aspect of the Seder as a Jewish symposium. It is Jewish not in the current ethnic use of that term. The Seder is a Jewish symposium in that it appropriates the world and the various interpretations of the world from its own perspective. Its celebration embodies its affirmations. It affirms the reality of Jewish historic existence in the world. In this sense the Passover Seder of the generations is a Jewish symposium on the Exodus from Egypt.

A SENSE OF GOD AND HISTORY

Two other Passover Haggadot merit attention. Achieving a sense of historical reality and the presence of God in that domain is not easy. The traditional Haggadah must have accomplished this. Its cherished use for more than a thousand years (parts are of two millennia duration), with its accretions such as its medieval songs and the many medieval manuscripts, some of them beautifully illuminated, give witness to the hold that its message had on the people. But both early on, in the eighth century C.E., and in the twentieth century, there were created two other Passover liturgical texts that merit attention.

THE KARAITE HAGGADAH

The Karaite Haggadah[40] stands in obvious contrast to the rabbinic Haggadah. Central to it is the Exodus from Egypt, and it contains many of the same biblical verses, sections, and psalms contained in the rabbinic Haggadah. But, except for a phrase and a blessing or two, no rabbinic passages are given in the Karaite Haggadah—no four questions, no four sons, no analysis of the numbers of plagues beyond the biblical ten (an analysis that starts with questions), no medieval songs.

Everything in the Karaite Haggadah, except for a phrase or two, is biblical. The biblical orientation of this Haggadah makes it a strange work. The absence of postbiblical Jewish texts makes for an absence of postbiblical Jewish existence. No sense of present time and place is presented in the Karaite Haggadah—no sense of movement, no awareness of exile. The Karaite Haggadah does not declare that "in every particular generation a person must see himself as if he went out of Egypt." Nor does it proclaim that "in every particular generation they rise against us to destroy us." This presents a curious paradox: while history is central to the Bible, the absence from the Karaite Haggadah of any postbiblical texts makes for a liturgical recitation that ignores history.

The lack of questions also serves to ignore history; for "the questioner . . . breaks through the horizon of sensory phenomenon; he transcends the immediate present."[41] Erwin Straus explains this breaking through the horizon of sensory phenomenon as enabling one "to gain distance."[42] This is clarified: "In asking questions and in discovering the means of answering his questions man emancipates himself from the confines of the immediate here and now; he knows where he stands, he understands his own particular position, he actualizes his freedom . . ."[43]

The absence of questions—the four questions, the four sons' questions, the questions of rabbis Jose, Eleazar, and Akiba concerning the number of plagues, the questions of why matzah and bitter herbs are eaten, the medieval song of number questions—makes for the absence of history in the Karaite Haggadah. Freedom, the great theme of Passover, is not delineated because only when a person asks questions is freedom actualized.

The absence of questions is more than an absence of rabbinic questions. There are no questions of any kind. In effect, no "attitude of interrogation," to borrow a phrase from Sartre, is

provided. This absence of questions is not accidental, but suggests something significant. In the rabbinic Haggadah one son
lacks the attitude of interrogation, the one who does not know
how to ask. He cannot "actualize his freedom." Erwin Straus
has indicated that "the act of questioning cannot be taught."[44]
The rabbinic Haggadah assumes this, too. It notes in connection
with this son, not that he should be stimulated to ask but that
"you open up [the issue] for him." One must assume that the
Karaites lacked the attitude of interrogation.

Not only does questioning enable one to break through the
sensory horizon but, as Straus indicated, "when man breaks
through the sensory horizon the moment becomes subordinate
to the future and the past in the whole of time."[45] The Karaite
Haggadah subordinates the present moment to the past. Ab-
solutizing biblical texts, lacking the questioning attitude, it has
no sense of the future.

THE SECULAR-ZIONIST HAGGADAH

How different is the Haggadah produced by *Ha-Shomer Ha-
Tzair*.[46] The opening thrust of this secular-Zionist Haggadah is
agriculturally oriented. A few verses from the Pentateuch and
Song of Songs are followed by bucolic verses by Moses ibn Ezra,
Jose ben Jose, Kalir, and Shlonsky stressing fertility and repro-
duction.

A strong sense of history is expressed in this Haggadah's use
of postbiblical literature. Passages from Frischman, Shlonsky,
Alterman, Bialik, Judah Ha-Levi, Song of the Partisans, Jeremiah,
Isaiah, and the traditional Haggadah are arranged in somewhat
haphazard order. The variety of sources and content, usually
identified, provides a sense of history, although this is somewhat
vitiated by bucolic illustrations on nearly every page.

In place of Kiddush, this secular-Zionist Haggadah begins with
a toast, "Let us raise the cup of salvation to Israel's Exodus from
exile to redemption." It then refers to this night's distinctiveness
and concludes with "the freeing of every man and nation from
its oppressors."

While there are no questions in this Haggadah, indeed, no
attitude of interrogation, it could not ignore the traditional four

questions. It reformulated them so that they became specifically Israeli and ambivalently secular:

Why is this night different from all other nights? On all other nights we eat hametz or matzah; this night only matzah. On all other nights children and parents relax *(m'subim)* separately; this night we relax together. On all other nights we dine briefly; this night we extend our meals and it is a night of watchfulness. On all other nights our talk is secular *(hulin)*; this night we keep talking about the Exodus from Egypt.

This last statement, distinguishing talk about the Exodus from secular speech, implies that Jewish history is sacred history. This is strange, because references to God are avoided in this secular-Zionist Haggadah except for a few biblical selections. There is a sense of sacred history, then, but no sense of the Holy One.

The only redeemer is Moses. Part of Exodus 3 is quoted in revised form. While in the desert, Moses is approached by an "angel of the Lord" and is told to go "to Egypt, to the afflicted and oppressed and tell them that they are slaves. But they will not understand . . . So force open their eyes . . . and redeem them . . . And you will be the father of a multitude of men and a leader of tribes. Of worms you will make men; of men, a nation; of sand, a land."

This Haggadah also has the traditional themes of "in every particular generation a person must see himself as if he went out of Egypt" and "in every particular generation the cry of Israel and the cry of those oppressed under their subjectors rises upward." It includes eschatological passages from a number of biblical books, a final toast, and the medieval song, "A kid for two farthings."

PAST-PRESENT-FUTURE

The Karaite Haggadah, lacking the interrogative attitude and lacking postbiblical material, lacks a sense of history. The secular-Zionist Haggadah, partly bucolic yet historically oriented, has a sense of sacred history but its Holy One is the Jewish people. It understands history as the arena of man's autonomy. It has only the four questions, no others. It does not truly break through "the horizon of sensory phenomenon"; for nearly halfway through the text it states, in a blocked-off square, leaving a space to be filled in with the present year:

> Now is the _____ year
> of our freedom,
> the freedom of Israel
> in the State of Israel.

The emphasis, then, of this secular-Zionist Haggadah is the contemporary. Unlike the rabbinic Haggadah's opening statement, "This is the bread of affliction which our ancestors ate in the land of Egypt . . . Now we are here; next year in the land of Israel. Now we are slaves; next year free men," which embodies a sense of past, present, and future, the secular-Zionist Haggadah tends to absolutize the present. It does not emancipate itself from the here and now.

The rabbinic Haggadah does just that, and therefore "the moment becomes subordinate to the future and to the past in the whole of time."[47] It embodies a philosophy of history. Its task is to show that there is meaning in Jewish history.

MEANING IN JEWISH HISTORY

The question of the meaning of Jewish history has always been with us. If it is true that "to ask earnestly the question of the ultimate meaning of history takes one's breath away; it transports us into a vacuum which only hope and faith can fill,"[48] the goal of the Seder is this: hope and faith in Jewish existence.

THE NEED FOR INTERPRETATION

The meaning of history is, obviously, not a simple issue. Karl Lowith clarifies that which has become opaque for us: "There would be no search for the meaning of history if its meaning were manifest in historical events."[49] Meaning in history, then, presupposes an interpretation of events. The events themselves do not give meaning.

Jewish tradition is involved with an interpretation of Jewish existence. Lowith discusses this:

There is only one very particular history—that of the Jews—which as a political history can be interpreted strictly religiously. Within the biblical tradition, the Jewish prophets alone were radical "philosophers of history" because they had, instead of a philosophy, an unshakable faith in God's providential purpose for his chosen people, punishing and rewarding them for disobedience and obedience. The exceptional fact of the Jewish existence could warrant a strictly religious understanding of political history, because only the Jews are a really historical people, constituted as such by religion, by the act of the Sinaitic revelation. Hence the Jewish people could and can indeed understand their national history and destiny as a religious-political unity. The eternal law which the Greeks saw embodied in the regular movement of the visible heavens was manifested to the Jews in the vicissitudes of their history, which is a story of divine, though most irregular, interventions . . . And, most amazing, the strength of this faith in a divine moral purpose in history rose to a climax just when all empirical evidence was *against* it . . . The very calamities of their national history strengthened and enlarged the prophetic faith in the sovereignty of the divine purpose; for He who sets empires in motion for judgment could use them for deliverance as well. The possibility of a belief in the providential ordering of world-historical destinies depends on this belief in a holy people of universal significance, because only peoples, not individuals, are a proper subject of history and only a holy people is directly related to the Lord as a Lord of history . . . [Therefore] the destiny of the Jews is a possible subject of a specifically Jewish interpretation . . . One has to conclude that a Jewish theology of history is indeed a possibility and even a necessity.[50]

The rabbinic Haggadah embodies past events, the present situation, and a sense of the future. The modern Jew's perception of the rabbinic Haggadah is that it emphasizes the past. In this sense the modern Jew is a Hellenic reader of the Haggadah. As Hermann Cohen noted, "To the Greeks history remains something we can know because it is a matter of fact [factum], that is, of the past."[51]

THE ESCHATOLOGICAL THRUST

If the modern Jew were to read the rabbinic Haggadah as a truly Jewish reader for whom "time becomes primarily future and future the primary content of our historical thought,"[52] he would grasp the eschatological thrust of the Haggadah. It has been rightly said that "in historical time we cannot draw the sharp dividing line between the functions of memory and action . . . the two are perpetually intertwined. Action is determined and guided by the historical consciousness, through recollection of the past, but on the other hand truly historical memory first grows from forces that reach forward into the future and give it form."[53]

The eschatological, then, is crucial for historical consciousness and action. The rabbinic Haggadah is nothing other than a proclamation, now, that "the past is a promise to the future."[54]

A NIGHT OF WATCHFULNESS

The Seder is conducted at night. The night is referred to as one of watchfulness: "It was a night of watching unto the Lord for bringing them out from the land of Egypt; this same night is a night of watching unto the Lord for all the children of Israel throughout their generations" (Exod. 12:42). The timing of the Seder is not incidental, and the initial four questions call attention to this night's difference from all other nights.

The concept of a sacred night is found in various traditions, but to understand this Passover night of watchfulness we must distinguish it from other traditions. The sacred night both in Christianity and in Islam is apparently influenced by Jewish tradition, therefore a relevant contrast is with the sacred night in Buddhism.

> In Buddhism on the holy night, Buddha received illuminations on the banks of the river Neranjara—that is to say, insight into the four noble truths and the path of liberation: "Here I have cut off the briars of passion from the tree of world being with the ax of reflection, and burnt them in the fire of knowledge; the stream of sensual desires has been dried up by the sun of knowledge; here

the eye of knowledge, in its purity, was opened for me and the fabric of madness rent; all the fetters of the existence of the world have been loosed for me." Failure to know and to comprehend the noble truths of suffering and its origin, of its suppression and the way leading to this, is the cause of the "loving and wandering on this long road."[55]

In Buddhism, then, night gives the insight that the apparently real world is not real. The fetters of existence of the world are loosened so that one might transcend the world.

The tradition of the night of watchfulness in Judaism is in direct opposition; the night of watchfulness makes possible precisely that which Buddha rejected, the wandering on the long road of exile and confronting the real world. The Targum on Exod. 12:42 reflects on nights in Jewish tradition:

> Four nights are recorded in the Book of Remembrance which is before the Master of the Universe: the first night when He revealed himself to create the universe; the second when He revealed himself to Abraham; the third when He revealed himself in Egypt; the fourth when He reveals himself to redeem the people of Israel from among the nations. All the nights are called nights of watchfulness.[56]

According to the Talmud, there are two opinions as to what a night of watchfulness means: one is that it was continuously watched for from the six days of creation; the other is that it is "a night which is under constant protection against evil spirits."[57] Most commentaries stress the latter interpretation, as does the Targum. Moderns who do not take evil spirits seriously can understand this traditional view if they interpret evil spirits as the realm of disorder, or chaos, which threatens order. Seder night, then, the night of order, stands in opposition to, and is protected against, disorder. The night is a night of entering into the order of history.

Staying awake is one of the concerns of the Haggadah. Tradition has held through the years that various devices should be used to keep the children alert during the Passover ceremony. The reference to the four sages who stayed up all night talking about the Exodus so that their students had to call them to morning prayers emphasizes this aspect of watchfulness. Both children and adults must remain awake.

The phenomenon of wakefulness has been studied:

> . . . the sleeper does not withdraw his interest from the world, as Freud said. Going to sleep, we completely surrender to the world, we abandon our stand opposite to it. Therefore, the sleeper is no longer free and able to conduct himself, and to stand his ground, to hold his own.[58]

In other words, the sleeper retreats to the purely biological realm; but being "Awake, we find ourselves within the world: we experience ourselves in the world together with the world, in relation to the world."[59] In the waking state, says Straus, we meet with others, while "the dreamer is alone in his dream world. No one else can ever enter it, nor can the dreamer leave it."[60]

The Seder, by stressing wakefulness, stresses freedom. Being awake for the Seder means being in the world, together with the world, in relationship to the world.

One reclines at the Seder. *M'subin,* usually translated "reclining," is a curious word. It is no exemplary gesture of the ancestors; for the Israelites leaving Egypt did not recline. *M'subin,* however, does not mean reclining, for reclining would be a midpoint modality between wakefulness and sleeping. *M'subin* should be understood as "seated around, inclining, bending forward." Inclination brings us closer to one another. Inclination, like leaning, means "'bending out' from the austere vertical."[61]

The night of watchfulness, then, is a sacred night of being wide awake, of questioning, of a community entering the order of history—truly the history feast par excellence of the world. Thus, the members of the Seder confront the world as a community of free men.

Chapter 3

SHAVUOT

THE CELEBRATION OF REVELATION

SHAVUOT HAS NOTHING like Passover's matzah and Seder, Succot's history hut, Rosh Ha-Shanah's shofar, or Yom Kippur's fast. Shavuot, celebrating the giving of the Torah, is a kind of a priori of all the holidays. Yet the Sinai event depends on the Exodus from Egypt. A continuity and close relationship exists, then, between Passover and Shavuot. The counting of the Omer between these two holidays is an aspect of this relationship. The Talmud's term for Shavuot, Azeret—that is, the conclusion of the Passover festival—calls attention to the interrelationship of these two holidays.

Modern students interpret the pilgrimage festivals as having originally been agricultural festivals subsequently restructured as history celebrations. The traditional view is the exact reverse. "Since our ancestors received the Torah at the conclusion of fifty days of exodus from Egypt, there was given to them the [holy] day of the first-fruit offering at the conclusion of the fifty days from the first day of Passover."[1] Shavuot is a festival in which a historic event is central. Even though the Jews for most of their historic existence were not farmers, they celebrated Shavuot as the festival of *Mattan Torah*, the giving of the Torah. A medieval sage noted, "When Israel is in exile and there is no cutting of the Omer, it must nevertheless celebrate the festival of Shavuot."[2]

RECTIFYING AN ANCESTRAL MISDEED

Shavuot has been celebrated, as have all Jewish holidays, with cessation from work, longer prayer services, and the study of Torah. Because Shavuot lacked a specific observance, the *Tikkun Layl Shavuot* was developed, an all-night vigil during which selections from Torah, written and oral traditions, were studied.

A reason was given for this Torah-study vigil. At Sinai, according to the tradition, the ancestors "slept all that night . . . the Holy One . . . found them sleeping and set up noisemakers . . . Moses awakened Israel and brought them to salute the King."[3] Because they slept through that night we, says a late commentator, "must rectify that, so as to show that we do not do such [things as the Exodus generation did]."[4] Thus, staying awake is a rectification of an ancestral misdeed. The tradition, critical of the ancestors, does not clarify, however, why the ancestral sleeping had to be rectified by the later generations.

SLEEPING AWAY TIME AND HISTORY

The phenomenon of being awake deserves analysis. Sleep is associated in Jewish tradition with death, and "the social nothingness of sleep implied by the comparison with death points to . . . absence of interaction [and to] social isolation."[5] Since the Torah is given to the covenantal community, social isolation or absence of interaction cannot be tolerated. The Torah is given to a people who are wide awake.

Two different times exist in human life: nocturnal or sleep time and diurnal or awake time. "Day time is . . . cumulative. The perception of self and others as growing, developing . . . refers to day time . . . Sleep-time . . . , predominantly noncumulative

. . . , becomes a redeemer from the fears associated with the passing of time and the definitive loss of the past . . ."⁶

Sleep time is the time of the archaic, ahistoric consciousness. It abolishes time and history. Obviously, sleep is a biological necessity. It is "the normal state of lower forms of animal life and of the human infant . . . wakefulness occurs [in these] when some specific *physiological* need is aroused . . ."⁷ This analysis leads to a conclusion significant for understanding *Mattan Torah* in the daytime: "The wakefulness of choice found in adult man is a new biological development."⁸ A mature, fully developed human being is a human being awake who has the possibility of choice and personal decision as against the animal and infant who are awakened only by physiological compulsion. *Mattan Torah* presupposes personal choice that characterizes the wide-awake adult human being.

The regressive aspect of sleep means "the suspension of historical continuity, the disintegration of spatial and temporal ordering, the vagueness of identity,"⁹ a state intolerable for Jewish existence. Central for Torah and its conception of reality is historical continuity and spatial-temporal ordering. Sharpness of identity is fundamental to Judaism. The true God must be distinguished from the gods. Covenantal Israel must remain separate from the nations. There is a sense of the past and future. The Jew's sustained awareness of Eretz Yisrael and the lands of diaspora is his spatial ordering. The central conception of this time-world and the coming time-world, the rhythm of the week, make up Judaism's temporal ordering.

AWAKE FOR ACOUSTICAL REVELATION

An analysis of the senses in the two times, sleep time and awake time, can deepen our understanding of *Mattan Torah*. During sleep, the most important activity is dreaming, during which "the temporal order disintegrates . . . [which] is why dream impressions are predominantly optical . . . But acoustic impressions, which require the sequence of time to form a whole, cannot, as fragmentary presences, be used by the dreamer to make up an encompassing meaningful unity."¹⁰

Revelation in Jewish tradition is primarily acoustical. The prophets who saw such things as a basket of summer fruit were asked by God what they saw, and what they saw was a paronomastic vision. God spoke the message. Even the grand vision of Ezekiel had no meaning until he heard the voice.

Mattan Torah is acoustic. The optical impressions, the thick cloud, lightning, and fire are secondary to the sound of the shofar (mentioned twice), and to God's and Moses' words. In Moses' final address the acoustic at Sinai is made emphatic: "You saw no matter of form" (Deut. 4:15).

On Sinai the covenantal community, having been aroused from sleep, not by physiological compulsion but by God and Moses, is alert for communication unlike the sleeper-dreamer who "is alone in his dream world . . . [since] communication is possible only in the state of awakeness."[11]

Along with being awake, "all communication, lingual included, is based in the being-with-another of mobility of meeting . . . in a common surrounding world."[12] This is true of *Mattan Torah* at Sinai. Mobility characterizes both God and the Children of Israel. The section of Scripture dealing with Sinai, Exodus 19, opens with a reference to Israel's travels and encampments. Throughout the chapter, movement occurs: God comes down upon the mountain; Moses and others ascend and descend the mountain.

Reflecting on communication "based in the being-with-another of mobility," Erwin Straus points out that "in primal and basic communication I am not a knower and the other is not the object of my communication . . . [nor] a thing singled out from a neutral background. I discover the other . . . as a partner . . . a being which can come near me . . ."[13] Straus understands this as "the power relationship of communication."[14] Power relationship is stressed in the Jewish sources dealing with Torah. The thunder, the lightning, the fire, the sound of the shofar are power realities. The people's response at Sinai, that they will hearken and do, are aspects of the people's power. The rabbinic term *m'pi ha-Gevurah*, "from the mouth of The Power," indicates how important power is in the giving of Torah.

STANDING UPRIGHT IN REALITY

The idea of the awakened people at Sinai has further implications. Erwin Straus explores for us the significance of the obvious; upon awakening, one is "ready to get up. In rising to an
erect position, and in the free movement upon the ground that
supports us, the objects appear. Erect and capable of movement
we can confront the other."[15] The erect posture characterizes the
Sinai situation, the rabbinic term for which is *Maamad Har Sinai,*
"the Stance at Mount Sinai." The rabbinic term is rooted in Scripture, where "standing" is repeated a number of times in Exodus
19 and Deuteronomy 4–5. In the aggadic work *Pirkei de Rabbi
Eliezer* it is reported that when Moses awakened the people he
said to them, "Stand up from your sleep for behold your God
desires to give the Torah to you."[16] Indeed, for the rabbinic mind,
standing connotes reality. Commenting on Deut. 29:14, "But with
him that standeth here with us this day before the Lord our God
and also with him that is not here this day," the midrash, sensitive
to the omission of "standing" in the second clause, says that
these "will one day be created; because there is not yet any
substance in them, the word 'standing' is not used with them."[17]

Not only the Israelites stood at Mount Sinai. God also stood,
according to the traditional *Mekilta de Rabbi Ishmael.*[18] *Maamad
Har Sinai* refers to both God and the people standing upright at
Mount Sinai.

STUDYING TORAH

The *Tikkun* of Shavuot night is the study of Torah. The study of
Torah, crucial for Jewish existence, must be understood on its
own terms. Despite the pragmatic bent of Jewish existence, its
eschewing theoretical speculation because it was of the opinion,
to quote Wittgenstein, that "learning is based on believing,"[19]
Torah was studied not only in order to fulfill the mitzvot. In a
curiously paradoxical way, study of Torah was more important
than observance of the mitzvot: "Observance depends on study,
not study on observance; the neglect of study is more serious
than nonobservance."[20]

TORAH AND STUDYING DEFINED

Torah study is often translated as study of the law. The term *Torah*, which includes laws, means *"teaching,"* and its connotations are as significant as its denotation. To translate *Torah* as "Law" is to misunderstand the Jewish tradition. In Western culture, " 'Law' . . . implies a submission which does not involve any spontaneity or countereffect on the part of the person subordinate to the law."[21] Torah, however, does involve countereffect, personal response, and commitment on the part of the covenantal community.

Study, too, needs to be understood. In America study is an aspect of career training usually confined to childhood, adolescence, and the early postadolescent years. Study, for the modern, is "book learning." The reading of newspapers is widespread in Western culture. Its importance was already appreciated in the nineteenth century by Hegel, who referred to reading the newspaper as "the morning prayer of the realist."[22] Reading novels and plays is also an important modern activity. Mircea Eliade has analyzed this:

> Reading includes a mythological function, not only because it replaces the recitation of myths in archaic societies and the oral literature that still lives in the rural communities of Europe but because through reading, the modern man succeeds in obtaining an "escape from time" comparable to the "emergence from time" effected by myths . . . Reading projects him out of his personal duration and incorporates him into other rhythms, makes him live in another "history."[23]

IMPORTANCE OF HEARING

Torah study, however, is not an activity of reading. It is hard work. According to the Mishnah there are forty-eight qualifications for acquiring Torah. Of these forty-eight, the visual—i.e., reading—is not mentioned. Mentioned, among other things, are "hearing of the ear, ordering of the lips . . . [being one] that hearkens and adds thereto."[24]

Torah study is primarily a recitation activity; thus it is acoustic rather than optical. Indeed, the phenomenon of revelation at

Sinai is oral. The Ten Commandments are traditionally referred to as the ten utterances. They were first spoken, and only subsequently given on stone tablets to Moses, who could risk breaking the tablets. Furthermore, the traditional view has been that the written Torah cannot be understood without the oral Torah also given at Sinai. To our time the rabbinic works are known as the Oral Torah.

The spoken word, not the written, is crucial for Jewish tradition. The ear, therefore, and not the eye, is the important organ. One or two examples will have to suffice. According to the midrash, God said, "Man has two hundred and forty-eight limbs, and the ear is but one of them; yet even though his whole body be stained with transgressions, as long as his ear hearkens [to the Torah] the whole body is vivified . . ."[25]

Not only aggadic texts consider the ear to be crucial; the halakic material also does. According to the Talmud, if someone cuts off another's arm,

> he must pay him for the value of the arm, and as to Loss of Time, the injured person is to be considered as if he were a watchman of cucumber beds; so also if he broke [the other's] leg, he must pay him for the value of the leg, and as to Loss of Time the injured person is to be considered as if he were a door-keeper; if he put out [another's] eye he must pay him for the value of his eye, and as to Loss of Time the injured person is to be considered as if he were grinding in the mill; but if he made [the other] deaf, he must pay for the value of the whole of him."[26]

David Cohen's *Kol Ha-Nevuah* is a study of the importance of hearing in the Jewish tradition in contrast to seeing in the Greek tradition.[27]

In this connection, too, we must address ourselves to the issue of the senses. "Sound, itself a dynamic fact, intrudes upon a passive subject. For the sensation of hearing to come about, the percipient is entirely dependent on something happening outside his control; and in hearing he is exposed to its happening."[28] That hearing depends on a happening means that hearing is a time event in contrast to sight, which "is unique . . . in beholding a contemporaneous manifold which may be at rest. All other senses construct their perceptual 'unities of a manifold' out of a temporal sequence of sensations which are in themselves time bound and nonspatial . . ."[29] In other words, hearing is a sense involved with time and "gives only dynamic and never static reality . . . not an object but a dynamical event at the focus of the object . . ."[30]

This clarifies the stress in the Sinai revelation on hearing rather than seeing. Torah is a dynamic event, and therefore there is temporal sequence. The dynamic event intrudes on the community. There is a sequence of sound as it comes to the people. It is significant that "objectivity emerges preeminently from sight;"[31] for, in contrast to this, the Sinai revelation is not concerned with objectivity. It is an event of intersubjectivity. It is a demanding situation, and it is not accidental that the tradition has it that God held the mountain, over the people, like a tank.[32]

THE COMPLEX FIELD OF DISCOURSE

The study of Torah has included the study of Talmud and the midrashim, commentaries, and codes. Jews are known as the people of the book. Yet Jews have not understood Torah study as a bookish activity. There were, in fact, profound reservations about writing down the Oral Torah. Only because of the fear of forgetting was the oral tradition recorded.

The modern who remains bound by the idea that the rabbinic works are books must be aware of the fact that the nature of a book is open to question. Michel Foucault, a reader and writer of many books, discusses this issue.

> The frontiers of a book are never clear-cut; beyond the title, the first lines, and the last full stop, beyond its internal configuration and its autonomous form, it is caught up in a system of references to other books, other texts, other sentences: it is a node within a network. And this network of references is not the same in the case of a mathematical treatise, a textual commentary, a historical account, and an episode in a novel cycle; the unity of the book, even in the sense of a group of relations, cannot be regarded as identical in each case. The book is not simply the object that one holds in one's hands; and it cannot remain within the little parallelepiped that contains it: its unity is variable and relative. As soon

as one questions that unity, it loses its self-evidence; it indicates itself, constructs itself, only on the basis of a complex field of discourse.[33]

The Talmud (and the works related to it) is not a series of books. It is, to use Foucault's excellent phrase, "a complex field of discourse." These rabbinic works are a five-hundred-year dialogue on the meaning of Torah. The commentaries and the supercommentaries, the glossators who at times conduct a polemic with the commentaries, are in essence a continuation of that long-enduring dialogue.

THE CENTRALITY OF QUESTIONS

Central to the Talmud are questions. Among the forty-eight ways in which Torah is acquired is the way of "[being one] that asks and makes answer."[34] On every page of the Talmud questions appear. Questions are so central that many a student of Talmud adds, when studying, "The Gemara asks . . . The Gemara answers." Questioning is indigenous to the Jewish tradition. As early as Genesis 3, God asks Adam questions: "Where art thou?" (v. 9) and "Who told thee that thou wast naked?" (v. 11). God also asks the woman questions. One of God's attributes, it would seem, is the "attitude of interrogation."[35] All of scripture presupposes questions. In connection with the Exodus, the pivotal event in the Torah, it is indicated that future generations will ask questions about Passover. The Jewish tradition embodies what a thinker, in another field of discourse, has called "a natural affinity with interrogation."[36]

Questions have been raised down the generations. One or two examples will serve. Judah the Pious, the central figure of the medieval German Hasidim, had been a frivolous youth until his father induced him to enter the *bet midrash* and study Torah. The first thing Judah does as he studies is to ask questions.[37] Even the eighteenth-century East European Hasidim, given to assuming that their faith was a simple faith, presupposed questions. "On Hoshannah Rabbah," they recorded, "every one prepared some question," based on a rabbinic text or some other work, "and the Baal Shem Tov's way was to answer [them] on this day."[38] A situation is described where a beloved son recites Torah before his father, who in turn raises various difficult questions. The father's motivation is not to confuse the son but to sharpen up things; this method is the "father's joy."[39]

While it is true that there is "the as yet unclarified matter of the hermeneutics of the question,"[40] we do have some inkling as to its function. Ludwig Feuerbach explained: "To ask a question and to answer are the first acts of thought. Thought originally demands two."[41] Thinking, then, presupposes what has been called the attitude of interrogation, and the attitude of interrogation is the dialogical attitude. According to Erwin Straus the goal of questioning is "to achieve a view of the comprehensive order . . . the questioner and person questioned direct themselves to the order of things."[42]

THE ORDER OF THINGS

Torah study has as its function directing the covenantal community to the order of things. The order of things is not a simple issue. "There is nothing more tentative . . . than the process of establishing an order among things; nothing that demands a sharper eye or a surer, better-articulated language . . . Order is at one and the same time that which is given in things as their inner law . . . and also that which has no existence except in the grid created by a glance, an examination, a language."[43]

This is both complex and crucial because "the fundamental codes of a culture—those governing its language, its schemes of perception, its exchanges, its techniques, its values, the hierarchy of its practices—establish for every man . . . the empirical orders with which he will be dealing and within which he will be at home."[44] The Jewish order of existence has always been particularly problematic. It had been attacked by the Babylonians, threatened by the Hellenized Syrians, shattered by the Romans, hated by the medieval anti-Semites, corroded by the Enlightenment, nearly destroyed by the Nazis. The Jewish community in exile for more than two thousand years faced the problem of maintaining and transmitting its fundamental codes. This has always been, even in the Land of Israel, the central problem; for the one nonautochthonous faith in the world was

Jewish faith. The very beginning of Jewish existence presupposes uprootedness. Abraham was asked to leave his native land. Egypt is not Israel's native land. *Mattan Torah* is not an autochthonous event. The greatest Jewish leader, Moses, was so nonautochthonous a leader that his birth, his life, his death, his burial all took place outside of the promised land. Every people has a native land; the Children of Israel have a Promised Land.

Since the Jewish order of existence has never been an autochthonous order, it is exceedingly fragile. Not rooted in a specific territory though always directed to it, always shifting its grid, the basic problem was how to maintain the Jewish order and transmit it down the generations. Only a nonautochthonous order has study central to it, not bookish study but dialogical study, a dialogical hermeneutics of the nonautochthonous event, *Mattan Torah.*

THE JEWISH CONSTRUCTION OF REALITY

According to the sociologist Peter Berger, "Like the other mammals, man is *in* a world that antedates his appearance. But unlike [them] . . . this world is not simply given, prefabricated for him. Man must *make* a world for himself . . . the condition of the human organism in the world is thus characterized by a built-in instability. Man does not have a given relationship to the world. He must ongoingly establish a relationship with it."[45]

This is true of all human beings. We suggest that Jewish existence, an existence that rejects the gods and thereby rejects the consensus of mankind, an existence lived in exile for the largest portion of its history, is particularly "characterized by a built-in instability." It is this nonautochthonous people that even in its most assimilationist days never completely "goes native," i.e., autochthonous, that of necessity studies Torah, its order of existence.

What is the function of order? According to Peter Berger, establishing order is establishing a "shield against terror." He explains, "the danger of meaninglessness . . . is the nightmare *par excellence* in which the individual is submerged in a world of disorder, senselessness and madness."[46] The study of Talmud, the six orders of covenantal existence, is nothing other than the

Jewish "construction of reality"[47] that serves as a shield against
the terror of exile's meaninglessness. Jewish thinkers were aware
of this. The Zohar states, "He who delights in Torah fears nothing,"[48] and explains, "Whoever is involved with Torah is not
afraid of evil spirits. He is guarded above. He is guarded below.
Furthermore, he subdues all the evil spirits in the world and
forces them down into the ultimate depths."[49] The Maharal of
Prague said that Torah is the *seder olam*, the order of the world.
The study of Torah would be nothing other than Jewish "universe
maintenance."[50]

Shavuot, then, has no specific observance. Central to it is Torah
study but this is central at all times. Shavuot, the celebration of
Mattan Torah, can have no other mitzvah. Its mitzvah is the
presupposition of all mitzvot: Torah study, the dialogical hermeneutics of God's Word.

Chapter 4

ROSH HA-SHANAH

THE DAY OF REMEMBRANCE

ROSH HA-SHANAH, the Jewish New Year celebration, is, according to tradition, the day on which the world was created.

Remembrances, *Zikhronot*, is one of the three motifs of the holiday. Remembrances refer to God's remembering creation, human deeds, the convenant with the ancestors, the Israelites following God in the wilderness, and the present community. That the present community is most important is implicitly indicated in the imperative form of a rabbinic text: "God says, 'Recite before me *Remembrances* so that remembrance of you may rise favorably before Me, and through what? Through the shofar.' "[1]

Remembrances are therefore connected with Soundings, *Shofarot*, another motif of Rosh Ha-Shanah. "Why do we blow on a ram's horn? The Holy One . . . said, 'Sound before Me a ram's horn so that I may remember on your behalf the Binding of Isaac

. . . and account it for you as if you had bound yourselves before Me.' "[2]

Remembrances and Soundings are connected with Kingship, *Malkhuyyot;* for God is King who remembers the Binding of Isaac on behalf of the community that sounds the ram's horn. Of these three themes of the New Year celebration, remembrance is central, for Rosh Ha-Shanah is called *Yom Ha-Zikkaron,* the Day of Remembrance.

REMEMBERING HISTORIC EVENTS

The need to remember implies the possibility of forgetting. Two historic events must not be forgotten: the Binding of Isaac and the Exodus. Other historic events are also not to be forgotten: Noah's having been saved, the destruction of Jerusalem and the Temple, the Exile.

Not all people remember historic events. In the Greek tradition, "Recollection does not seek to situate events in a temporal frame but to reach the depths of being, to discover the original, the primordial reality from which the cosmos issued."[3] This is also the "structure of popular memory," the concerns of which are "categories instead of events, archetypes instead of historic personages . . . The memory of the collectivities is anhistorical."[4]

Jewish memory, however, does not focus on being, categories, or archetypes. Jewish memory focuses on historic persons and historic events. These have survived in Jewish memory for three and a half millennia.

ANCESTORS, NOT ARCHETYPES

The ancestors are not archetypes but historic persons. Each patriarch-matriarch couple is different from the other two. Moses, the prophets, the judges, and kings are each different from one another. The "archaic consciousness . . . [which] preserves only what is exemplary"[5] could not understand the rabbinic statement that the shofar is sounded so that God "may remember the Binding of Isaac . . . and account it for you as if you had bound yourselves before Me." The Binding of Isaac never became an exemplary gesture to be reenacted. The *As If* of the rabbinic observation is a denial of the exemplary gesture of the archaic consciousness. When the liturgy refers to the Binding of Isaac, or when the shofar is sounded, the congregation does not reenact the Binding. Furthermore, the shofar that serves to remind God of the Binding is the horn of a ram, the animal sacrificed in Isaac's stead. The archaic consciousness would not do what Jewish historic consciousness does: use an object in the biological order to remember an event in the order of history. Indeed, the Binding of Isaac, unique to this patriarch, was itself an *As If*. For at the penultimate moment when Abraham was told not to sacrifice Isaac, he was also told "thou hast not withheld thy son."[6] The Binding, therefore, was nothing other than *As If* Abraham had sacrificed Isaac. It was a nonenactment of a sacrifice. This unique nonenactment is never reenacted as exemplary gesture.

THREE INTENTIONS OF MEMORY

Rosh Ha-Shanah as the Day of Remembrance is to be understood in terms of memory in Jewish tradition. In Hebrew "to remember" implies "an effect on the totality and direction of will . . . therefore *Zakhor* may also mean to begin an action . . . to proceed to do something."[7] An observation by the philosopher Ernst Cassirer clarifies this. "Action," says Cassirer, "is determined and guided by the historical consciousness through the recollection of the past but . . . historical memory first grows from forces that reach forward into the future and give it form."[8] Cassirer stresses the future aspect of memory: "One of the most essential achievements of memory is to be found in expectation, in direction toward the future."[9]

This expectative quality of memory, what has been called "prospective memory,"[10] is one of the three intentions of memory: intention toward the earlier, toward the now, and toward the later.[11] These three intentions of memory are embodied in the traditional liturgy of Rosh Ha-Shanah. Even Saadia Gaon's ten reasons for sounding the shofar express these three intentions:

There are ten reasons why the Creator, be blessed, commanded us to blow the ram's horn on Rosh Ha-Shanah. The first reason is, because Rosh Ha-Shanah marks the beginning of Creation, on which the Holy One, be blessed, created the world and reigned over it . . .

The second reason is that, since Rosh Ha-Shanah is the first of the ten days of Teshuvah, the ram's horn is blown to announce their beginning, as though to warn: Let all who desire to turn in Teshuvah, turn now . . .

The third reason is to remind us of our stand at the foot of Mount Sinai . . . in order that we may take upon ourselves that which our forefathers took upon themselves when they said [Exod. 24:7] "We will do and obey . . ."

The fourth reason is to remind us of the words of the prophets which are compared to a ram's horn . . .

The fifth reason is to remind us of the destruction of the Temple and the battle alarms of the foe . . . when we hear the sound of the ram's horn, we beseech God to rebuild the Temple.

The sixth reason is to remind us of the Binding of Isaac . . . so ought we to be ready . . . for the sanctification of His name . . .

The seventh reason is . . . that we fear and tremble and bend our will to the Will of the Creator . . .

The eighth reason is to remind us of the Great Day of Judgment that we may fear it . . .

The ninth reason is to remind us of the gathering of the dispersed of Israel, that we may passionately long for it . . .

The tenth reason is to remind us of the revival of the dead that we may believe in it . . .[12]

Creation, the Binding of Isaac, the Sinai Assembly, Prophetic Words, and the Destruction of the Temple are intentions toward the earlier. The Ten Days of Penitence and Bending to God's Will are intentions toward the now. Judgment Day, the Ingathering of Israel, and the Revival of the Dead are intentions toward the future.

NOTING WHAT IS MISSING

Since Rosh Ha-Shanah is the day on which the world was created, the liturgy includes references to creation. One might have expected, therefore, that the Torah readings would be the account of creation in Genesis. Creation texts were recited at the New Year's celebration in other cultures. In Babylon, for example, "On the evening of the fourth day of the New Year celebration, the Epic of Creation [Enuma Elish] . . . was recited in the Temple, for each New Year shared something essential with the first day when the world was created and the cycles of seasons started."[13] And "The recital of the god's victory over chaos at the beginning of time cast a spell of accomplishment over the hazardous and all-important renewal of natural life in the present."[14]

Significantly, the biblical account of Creation is not recited on Rosh Ha-Shanah. Unlike the Babylonian New Year festival, Rosh Ha-Shanah shares nothing essential with the first day of creation. The Babylonian intention at the recitation of its creation epic was "the abolition of time, the restoration of primordial chaos, the repetition of the cosmogenic act."[15] Its goal was "to abolish history."[16] Abolishing history "betoken[s] archaic man's refusal to accept himself as a historical being, his refusal to grant value to memory and hence to unusual events (i.e., events without an archetypal model) that . . . constitute duration . . . In all these [cosmogonic] rites and [in] all these attitudes is the will to devaluate time."[17] The Torah readings for Rosh Ha-Shanah relate the birth and Binding of Isaac; the prophetic readings recount the birth of Samuel and the political crisis in the time of Jeremiah. History is never abolished.

It has often been noted that it is surprising that *Yizkor*, the prayer for the remembrance of the dead, is not recited on Rosh Ha-Shanah. Various explanations have been offered for this omission. We suggest that the recitation of *Yizkor* does not fit in with the structure of intentions of Rosh Ha-Shanah. Each Jewish celebration embodies a configuration in which each observance or prayer is part of the larger gestalt. Omissions, therefore, are not accidental. It is in the pattern of Rosh Ha-Shanah that *Yizkor* must not be recited. For the archaic mentality, the

> eternal repetition of the cosmogenic act . . . permits the return of
> the dead to life and maintains . . . the belief . . . [that] the dead
> return to their families (. . . often . . . as "living dead") at the New
> Year season . . . [It expresses] the hope that the abolition of time
> is possible at this mythical moment . . . The dead can come back
> now, for all barriers between the dead and the living are now
> broken.[18]

Traditional Judaism's affirmation of the resurrection of the dead in the future does not, however, abolish time and does not break the barriers between the dead and the living. On the contrary, Rosh Ha-Shanah is a time of Judgment when God decides who will live and who will die. Its great cry is "Remember us unto life." Asserting the barriers between life and death, it avoids remembering the dead. On Yom Kippur, which is not the day of creation and is not, therefore, open to the risk of the archaic consciousness that returns the dead to their families, *Yizkor* is recited.

BOTH GOD AND THE PEOPLE REMEMBER

Explicit in the liturgy of the Day of Remembrance is the theme that two remember: God and the People of Israel. What does it mean that God remembers? "The essence of God's remembering lies in his acting toward someone because of a previous commitment."[19] The previous commitment is the covenant between God and the People of Israel. The Covenant was made in the past but it is of the present and is to continue in the future. God is called upon to remember Israel because the one that God "does not remember has no existence."[20] Asking God to remember is, therefore, Israel's plea for its existence, because Israel's existence depends upon God. God's memory "is not a recreating of the past but a continuation of the selfsame purpose"[21] of the past, the covenantal relationship that God has with the covenantal community. Indeed, "God's memory encompasses His entire relationship with His people. His memory includes both the great deeds of the past as well as His continual concern for the future."[22]

That the People of Israel call upon God to remember presupposes, of course, their remembering. What does this mean? Israel's memory "serves in making Israel noetically aware of a history which is ontologically a unity . . . By linking herself to the past Israel becomes part of the future because past and future are one in God's purpose."[23] To be noetically aware, to link oneself to the past, does not mean passivity. As we have noted, to remember, in Hebrew, can also mean "to begin an action . . . to proceed to do something." That *something* merits consideration.

Remembering, *ZKR* in Hebrew, "comes to mean recognition or discernment which turns one to God . . . a genuine reaching out after a reality, which in the very act becomes a new and living present . . . Memory as a recalling of the past with discernment approaches the act of repentance."[24] "Discernment" is significant because it "emphasizes obedience in the future."[25]

For the People of Israel to remember is the beginning of repentance. That is why Rosh Ha-Shanah, the beginning of the Ten Days of Repentance, is called the Day of Remembrance, for memory begins the act of repentance.

Remembering is the discernment that turns one to God. Turning, *teshuvah*, is the proper term. Repentance stresses the inward; it connotes feeling sorry, an inner emotional state. *Repentance* comes from a word meaning regret.[26] Turning, *teshuvah*, is not simply an inner emotional state, nor is it an outer, detached, impersonal state. *Teshuvah* is an act, a movement of the whole person and an act, a movement, of the covenantal community; a returning to God in the arena of the everyday world.

Chapter 5

YOM KIPPUR

THE DAY OF FORGIVENESS

YOM KIPPUR, known as the Day of Atonement, is the Jewish year's most solemn day, characterized by prohibitions, restraints, and confessions of sins. It is also a day of hope. Confession of sins is accompanied by the hope that the sins will be forgiven. As there are many references to many sins, the day is called *Yom Ha-Kippurim*, the Day of Forgivenesses (of the many sins).[1]

On this day of high consciousness of having sinned, no reference is made either to Adam's sin (i.e., primal sin) or to a state of sin. Although Adam's sin was of consequence, according to the tradition, his sin is not a paradigm for the Jew.

THE COVENENTAL COMMUNITY CONFESSES

Sinful deeds are confessed during the late afternoon prayer service before the pre–*Yom Ha-Kippurim* meal, and ten times during the services of the Day of Forgivenesses. Each confession is actually two confessions. One, the Short Confession, *Viduy Zuta*, is composed of twenty-five verbs (four of which are double words) for sinning. The other, the Great Confession, *Viduy Rabbah*, refers to forty-four sins, to which is added a list of deserved punishments for sins, about which forgiveness is asked.

These two confessions are expressed in the plural: "We have sinned." Every verb in the Short Confession and in the Great Confession has the suffix "we." Not that every individual has committed every sin. Each person confesses both his/her own sinful acts and everyone else's sinful acts. It is the covenantal community that confesses and asks to be forgiven.

The confessions do not make the traditional distinction between sins committed against one's fellows and sins committed against God. Every statement in the Great Confession refers to a sin that "we" have committed "before Thee." All sins, including those that harm one's neighbor, are sins against God.

NEITHER SINFUL BEING NOR ENDLESS LIST

This communal confession presents a problem: How is it possible to confess all the particular sins that anyone in the covenantal community may have committed without reciting an endless list of offenses? And how is it possible to avoid the conception of a state of sin, of sinful being, unless there is an infinite catalog of sins?

Both confessions solve this dilemma. The Short Confession's twenty-five verbs include general terms such as "we have been faithless" and specific ones such as "we have robbed." Structured as an alphabetic acrostic, these terms impart a sense of the totality of sinful acts since the confession is both general and specific.

The Great Confession, too, is neither a statement of sinful being nor an endless list of sins. This confession, also using the alphabetic acrostic form, refers to the particular human organs that have acted sinfully, to some broadly stated sinful acts, and to particular punishments for sins. For example, the mouth has sinned. Except for "the sin of food and drink," no doubt referring to the ingestion of nonkosher food, the sins of the mouth refer to various sins of speech, some of which are subsequently specified. Hand and foot have sinned. The heart has sinned. The eyes have sinned. Other parts of the body have sinned—for example, the forehead (i.e., arrogance). Although the sexual organs are not mentioned, specific sins of a sexual nature, such as incest, are.

Also confessed are sins of a particular personal situation: sins committed under compulsion, sins committed out of ignorance, and sins intentionally committed; sins committed in error, sins committed willingly and unwillingly, publicly or privately, and those done presumptuously. Sins of deliberate deceit are confessed: ensnaring neighbor and wronging neighbor. Bribery, extortion, interest-taking, and causeless hatred are also confessed.

AN AUDIBLE RECITATION

Both the Short Confession and the Great Confession must be recited audibly; the silence of the contrite heart does not suffice.[2] There is reason behind the speaking forth of the confession. "Speech, while connecting the speaker and listener, keeps them, at the same time, at a distance."[3] The confessions are made before God; the words serve both to connect the confessor with God the listener and to keep the two at a distance from each other. For God is the Judge, and a judge must maintain distance in order to judge. Standing aside from the sins of the past, the confessor, too, gains distance and is able to face up to the enormity of these sins.

CONFESSED WHILE STANDING

These sins must be confessed while one is standing.[4] Standing is a mode of Jewish piety, from the day of *Maamad Har Sinai* (the Stance at Mount Sinai) throughout the time of the Jerusalem Temple where all the services were performed while standing, and in post-Temple times to our own day when the Amidah prayer is recited three times each day and five times during the

Yom Ha-Kippurim holiday. The upright posture is "a specific mode of being in the world."[5] It is the posture of confession. As speech keeps speaker and listener at a distance from each other, so, too, "the upright posture produces . . . distance . . . puts us opposite to things, confronts us with one another."[6] We stand opposite to God and are confronted by God. That is the reason, it would seem, that one must not prostrate oneself while confessing.[7] While standing and confessing the head is bent. This is an expression of reverence;[8] the upright posture "does not change even if the head is tilted."[9] Indeed, according to a psychologist, "Guilt tends to cause the person to hang his head lower."[10] Standing, it can be said, is the *Yom Ha-Kippurim* mode of being in the world.

THE HISTORICAL EVENT OF PARDON

This holiday seems to be an exception in the scheme of Jewish holidays that are rooted in historic events. Many think of this day as an escape from history and, therefore, an escape from the particular to the universal and from the material to the spiritual (no bodily pleasures are permitted in the observance). The tradition that structures this holiday does not, however, interpret it this way.

Two traditions point to historical events. One tradition holds that this is the day on which Joseph's brothers sold him into slavery.[11] The day's liturgy refers to this. A second tradition maintains that on this day Moses descended Mount Sinai with the second set of the Tablets of the Decalogue and announced the glad tidings of reconciliation between God and the Israelites, the granting of pardon for the sin of the golden calf.[12] The Day of Forgivenesses celebrates this historic event of reconciliation.

REMEMBERING JOSEPH

In connection with the theme of Joseph being sold into slavery, a special liturgical composition known by the rubric *These I Remember* is recited. The liturgy prepares the congregation for this recital by descriptions of the high priest's sacrificial service in Temple times. There is a litany of counting the high priest's sprinkling of the blood of the day's sacrifice, a recitation of the procedures he followed. His prostrations are enacted as the congregation recites them. The high priest's appearance on leaving the Holy of Holies and the joy of those who beheld his glowing face are described. Passages follow referring to the iniquity of the ancestors that caused the destruction of the Temple, to our sins that delay its restoration, a lament on the lack of leadership, of high priest, of altar, of sacrificial system. References are made to our contemporary misery and to a hope for restoration of relationship with God.

REMEMBERING THE TEN MARTYRS

This leads to the recitation of the martyrology *These I Remember* because the martyrdom was an event that served to compensate for the sin of selling Joseph into slavery. The martyrology, about which historical scholarship has raised critical questions,[13] is a text of profound pathos. It is of the utmost importance in the liturgy of this day. A similar text recited on the Ninth of Av is a litany of destruction. On the Day of Forgivenesses this martyrology is a litany of sacrifice.

These I Remember tells of a unique, most holy sacrifice: the sacrifice of the Ten Holy Sages. The central figure in this martyrology is the high priest, Rabbi Ishmael. At the request of the nine saintly sages, he ascended the heavens and learned that it was Heaven's decree that they be martyred. He so informed his colleagues.

Simon ha-Nasi was the first to be executed, as he had hoped, for he did not want to witness the death of R. Ishmael, "the one who serves the One Who dwells in the Temple." As R. Ishmael laments Simon's death, the lamentation calls him to the attention of the Roman tyrant's daughter. Lusting for the handsome priest, she asks that he be spared. Denied this, she asks that his face be flayed and given to her. R. Ishmael cries out to God. In answer to an angel's bitter plea as to whether this is the reward of Torah study, a Heavenly Voice, threatening to destroy the world should there be another complaint, asserts "this is My Decree."

More attention (we have omitted much) is devoted to the martyrdom of R. Ishmael than to the other nine martyrs because the high priest, the only one who performs the sacrificial service on the Day of Forgivenesses, is himself the sacrificial victim. This accounts, too, for the theme of his being handsome, an incongruous note in a martyrology. Parallel to the people's noting the glow and beauty of the high priest's face as he leaves the Holy of Holies, the tyrant's daughter notes the attractiveness of the high priest who is the sacrificial victim.

The martyrdom is ultimately a sacrifice, according to an old tradition that "the righteous ones are sacrificed on a heavenly altar before the Holy One, Blessed Be He."[14] That ten were martyred is in keeping with the tradition that ten brothers sold Joseph into slavery and with the tradition that "for any manifestation of sanctification [*kedushah*, a term also used in connection with martyrdom], not less than ten is required."[15]

Despite the fact, then, that there is now no altar, no high priest, no sacrifice, there has been a sacrifice so total—ten saintly sages, including a high priest, were sacrificial victims—that the sin of the ten brothers is forgiven.

A CONTRASTING CONFESSIONAL TEXT

Another confessional text, not recited in more than two millennia, merits reflection by virtue of contrast with the traditional Jewish confessions. This archaic confessional text is recorded in what is known as *The Egyptian Book of the Dead*.[16] Among its forty-two sins are iniquity, violent robbery, fornication, stealing, murder, lying, causing a man to weep, and baiting fish with bait made from fish. There is in this confession a great sensitivity to the human dimension and to the natural dimension. Cultic sins are also listed. Indeed, some interesting parallels can be drawn between the Jewish Great Confession and the Egyptian Confession of the Dead. That each lists some forty or so sins is an intriguing coincidence.

The differences between these two confessions, however, are of the utmost importance. The Egyptian confessor is dead. Through his confession, he seeks eternal life in another realm. The Egyptian confession reads in the first person singular; it is not a communal confession. A most significant difference, one not of degree but of kind, is that the Egyptian confession is a negative one while the Jewish confession is a positive one. The Egyptian confesses nothing. He, deceased, declares that he has *not* committed any of the listed sins. He does not proclaim his guilt but his innocence. He repents of nothing. The Egyptian *Negative Confession of the Dead* is nothing other than a magic formula that enables the deceased to enter a new domain. The Jew, however, confesses his or her sins and the sins of the community.

HEARING SCRIPTURE

The Afternoon Service of *Yom Ha-Kippurim* includes a reading from the Pentateuch, Lev. 18:1-30, followed by a recitation of the book of Jonah. This prophetic portion, decided on (as are all scriptural readings) by the rabbinic tradition, was both inevitable and unexpected. Inevitable because it is the one biblical book that deals with the repentance of an entire community; unexpected because it deals with the repentance of a gentile, pagan community. No other city in scripture, not even Jerusalem, is depicted as repenting. The recitation of *Jonah* teaches the power of repentance.

THE CLOSING OF THE GATES OF PRAYER

The *Neilah* ("closing") service concludes the Day of Forgivenesses. By tradition the congregation remains standing during this entire service of the closing of the gates of prayer.

The Great Confession is not recited during this final service. References to sinning are not excluded—the Short Confession is recited—but a greater emphasis is put on God's mercy and willingness to pardon. This is expressed in the recitation of the prayer *Almighty King* who grants pardon to sinners and forgiveness to transgressors, and does not treat them according to their wickedness. Some five times the congregation, referring to God's having instructed them to recite the thirteen Attributes of Mercy, recites Exod. 34:5-7, "And the Lord descended in the cloud and stood with him there and proclaimed the name of the Lord. And the Lord passed by before him and proclaimed: 'The Lord, the Lord, God, merciful and gracious, long suffering, and abundant in goodness and truth; keeping mercy unto the thousandth generation, forgiving iniquity and transgression and sin, and holding [the people] guiltless . . .' " The *Neilah* service concludes with the prayer *Our Father, Our King* and the "Hear O, Israel . . ." proclamation, the thrice-proclaimed "Blessed be the Name of His Glorious Majesty for ever and ever," followed by "The Lord, He is God," proclaimed seven times. The shofar is sounded. The evening prayers are recited. The fast is broken.

GREAT TENSIONS IN THE SABBATH OF SABBATHS

This day is a holiday celebrated in the form of prayer in the synagogue. Indeed it is so much a synagogue celebration rather than home celebration that in the middle ages (and perhaps even in our time) some have spent the entire night in the synagogue reciting psalms.

The liturgy of the Day of Forgivenesses is particularly rich with allusions to midrashic literature about the patriarchs and their deeds, their faithfulness to God, their trials and tribulations. The patriarchs and their descendants are held in critical esteem, for as the introductory statement of the Short Confession has it, "We and Our Forefathers have sinned."

The Day of Forgivenesses embodies polarities. It is the Sabbath of Sabbaths. Yet while Sabbath is the time for good food and sexual intimacy, on this day these are rigorously prohibited. On Sabbath there is no liturgical mention of sins because Sabbath is a foretaste of redemption; but on the Sabbath of Sabbaths sins are confessed ten times.

Fasting is central to this day. The two pentateuchal portions recited in the morning, Leviticus 16 and Num. 29:7-11, refer to the fast. Yet the prophetic recitation that follows, Isa. 57:14–58:14, expresses criticism of fasting. The prophetic criticism of fasting is recited because of the rabbinic tradition that determined all scriptural readings, since scripture itself does not decree any scriptural readings. This rabbinic tradition of pentateuchal readings on fasting and a prophetic reading critical of fasting also determined the reading of the Book of Jonah, which tells of the people of Nineveh who, together with their cattle, follow the king's decree, fast, and thereby repent of their sins.

These polarities make for great tensions. Refraining from all food and drink for somewhat more than twenty-four hours, a strenuous enterprise, is undercut by prophetic criticism. And prophetic criticism, in turn, is undercut by a prophetic book that tells of the fasting of the repentant pagan city. This Day of Forgivenesses is a holiday, a Sabbath of Sabbaths, during which all appetites are denied. All claims are undercut, for one has no claims on God as the covenantal community confesses its sins and thereby hopes for God's forgivenesses.

Chapter 6

SUCCOT

SPACE IN HISTORY

SUCCOT IS THE Jewish holiday that has the largest and most
carefully constructed artifact, the succah. The succah is essen-
tially a covering or roof; obviously, there can be no roof without
walls. The size of the succah and the area covered are discussed
in the Talmud and regulated in the codes. The covering must
be constructed of natural material—natural material detached,
however, from the ground. The succah cannot be a natural en-
closure, but must be a humanly constructed shelter. " 'Thou shalt
make' (Deut. 16:13) [implies] but not from that which is already
made."[1]

Jews are to dwell in succot so that they "may know" that God
"made the children of Israel to dwell in booths when I brought
them out of the land of Egypt" (Lev. 23:43). Yet it is not clear,
even to the sages of the Talmud, what these booths in the wilderness were. One sage was of the opinion that the booths were

covered by clouds of God's glory, i.e., not human artifacts. Another sage was of the opinion that they were "real booths," i.e., human artifacts.[2] Their uncertainty is not surprising, for Scripture is silent on the matter of domiciles in the desert. While food problems—water, manna, quail—are noted, nothing is said about living quarters.

Modern scholars have interpreted Succot as having originally been an agricultural festival, the hut a farmer's booth in the field. As if sensing this view, traditional thinkers insisted on distinctions.

> Even though we went out of Egypt in the month of Nissan, He [God] did not command us to make succot at that time. For it is summer time, and it is the practice of everyone to make succot for shade. Consequently, it would not be noticed that we [Jews] make them at the command of God. He commanded us, therefore, to make them in the seventh month, the time of the rains. The usual practice is for everyone to leave his succah for his house. But we [Jews] go out of the house so as to dwell in the succah. This way it is demonstrated that one makes [the succah] for the sake of God's commandments.[3]

The traditional commentators reflect on the question of the season. We reflect on the structure.

NEITHER DREAM HUT NOR COSMOLOGICAL HOUSE

Gaston Bachelard, a twentieth-century French philosopher, has written *The Poetics of Space*,[4] a study that deals with natural and man-made enclosures. His analysis can give us insight to the succah by virtue of contrast.

His "dwelling" is the *oneiric house* and the *dream hut*, the "legendary images . . . the dream of a thatched cottage or . . . of a hermit's hut[5] . . . which transcends everything that has been seen, even everything that we have experienced personally."[6] And "the hermit is *alone* [Bachelard's emphasis] before God . . . [in] a universe outside the universe. The hut . . . possesses the felicity of intense poverty."[7]

Outside space and time, the legendary hut is outside the ordinary world. It is found in the world of reverie. Indeed, Bachelard's final work, *The Poetics of Reverie*, serves as a commentary on his hut.

For Bachelard, "reverie . . . helps us escape time, make[s] us recognize within the human soul the permanence of a nucleus of childhood . . . a childhood outside history."[8] He values "the great *once upon a time* which we relive by dreaming in our memories of childhood . . ., the world of the *first time* . . . that lives within us [and is] not a memory of history but a memory of the cosmos. *Times when nothing happened* [his emphasis] came back."[9]

To achieve this, "we must desocialize our memory,"[10] which leads to "detemporalization."[11] Bachelard's ultimate option is "life without events, a life which does not mesh with the lives of others;" since "it is the lives of the others which bring events into our life."[12]

These views are, rather surprisingly, the views of what have been called the archaic societies. Mircea Eliade has studied "their revolt against concrete, historical time, their nostalgia for a periodical return to mythical time for the beginning of things."[13] Bachelard wants to escape time just as archaic man is involved with "the abolition of time."[14]

The archaic societies that, like Bachelard, wanted to abolish time, did nevertheless build actual huts that served as sacred space. The sacred hut was built on the plan of a model received in a dream. Among the Delaware Indians it was known as the Big House, built of logs placed horizontally, with an earthen floor, a roof made of shingles, and two smoke holes. "Of ceremonial significance was the oaken centerpost which supported the ridgepole and which bore two large carvings of the human face—one facing east, the other west. The faces represented . . . the masked spirit who was keeper of the game."[15] The Big House represented "the universe; its floor, the earth; its four walls the four quarters, its vault the sky dome."[16]

The prescribed rituals were performed at night. Men and women, wearing their best clothing, their faces ritualistically painted, sat separately and were silent until they participated in the ceremony. "Those gifted with a vision or dream, and hence in communication with the supernatural world, were called upon to recite their visions."[17] An important ceremony was the ritual of kindling new fires that were kept burning during the recitations. The floor was repeatedly swept "to clear a path to heaven . . . There was dancing around the centerpost which symbolized the tie between the Creator and the Earth."[18]

According to a native, the origin of the Big House "was long ago in the beginning."[19] The purpose of the ceremony was "to avert physical catastrophe."[20] If the ceremony were not performed regularly "the world might come to an end."[21]

A DWELLING IN HISTORY

The succah is neither Bachelard's dream hut nor the cosmological house of the archaic societies. There are at least two different opinions as to the reason for a succah. One has been noted above. A second has been recorded by Eleazar of Worms (d. between 1223 and 1232), mystic, halakist, and author of *Sefer Ha-Rokeach*. He wrote as follows:

> There are those that interpret it that when they [the Israelites] besieged the land of the Amorite, of Sihon and Og, and the cities of the land of Canaan, then Israel dwelt in succot as it is written, "And the Ark and Israel and Judah abide in succot" (2 Sam. 11:11). For in the field (of battle) He gave them cover until they conquered Rabbah of the Ammonites. So [too] Israel [was given cover] until they conquered Canaan. This is the [meaning of] "that I made the children of Israel dwell in booths" [i.e.], when they besieged the nations.[22]

This interpretation of dwelling in succot fits in with the first interpretation, which refers to dwelling in the wilderness after the Exodus from Egypt, on the way to the Land of Israel. The interpretation recorded by R. Eleazar stresses the conquest of the Land. Both conceive the succah not as cosmological hut nor as oneiric house but as dwelling in history. This historic hut is involved with events and therefore with others. Eighteenth- and nineteenth-century pictures of succot showing the family meal,[23] succot in crowded quarters such as *Meah Shearim* in Israel, contemporary American succah "hopping" (making the rounds of

various succot), indicate lives meshed with others. Succot are
not Bachelard's huts of hermits alone before God. From the time
of the Talmud when Queen Helena of Adiabene and her sons
dwelt in a succah visited by rabbinic sages,[24] through the time
of Moses Mat (c. 1555–1606), a Galician rabbi who discussed the
commandment of sleeping with one's wife in the succah,[25] the
succah has been no hermit's hut of solitude. Nor, with its dec-
orations, ornaments, and wall paintings,[26] does it embrace Bachelard's felicity of poverty. For the succah, events—the Exodus
and the conquest of the Land—are central. For the succah, memories of the Exodus and the conquest are socialized. The events
and the memories are those of the Children of Israel.

NO PRESCRIBED RITUALS

There are no prescribed rituals to be performed in the succah—
no kindling of sacred fires, no smoke holes in the roof, no ritual
sweeping of the floor, no recitation ritual. Even the *Ushpizin*[27]
recitation is not a cosmological recitation but a brief prayer asking
among other things that God grant food and water to those in
need and a dinner invitation to seven historic persons: Abraham,
Isaac, Jacob, Joseph, Moses, Aaron, and David. No myths, stories, or visions are recited in the succah. Only one activity takes
place in the succah: dwelling, defined as eating, drinking, and
sleeping.[28] The succah is therefore a particular kind of habitation
in history. There is no central pole in the succah to serve as the
axis mundi, the world axis. There is no *cosmic* orientation to the
succah. The succah is not a microcosm. It does not duplicate a
primal prehistoric hut or even the booth in the wilderness, for
no one is certain what the booth in the wilderness was.

NO PATTERN OF CONSTRUCTION

According to Mordecai Ha-Cohen of Safed, sixteenth-century
mystic, it is obvious that the succah of the wilderness is not the
paradigm for the succah of the generations. According to Mordecai Ha-Cohen, "The Holy One, Blessed be He, said, 'Even
though I command you to make a succah in remembrance of
the succot in which I settled you, it is impossible [for you] to

make ones like those that I made that were of clouds of [My]
Glory . . . because the succah of a human being is not like the
succah of the Holy One, Blessed be He; so, too, it is impossible
to make it in the same time that I [originally] made it for you.
For I made it when you were in the wilderness in a place where
there was no fig tree nor vine nor shady tree.' "[29]

Not only is the succah erected by each generation different
from the first succah, but the succah of the generations is different from what might be called the eschatological succah, the
succah of the future. There is a very old tradition of an eschatological succah. Two different terms are used for the succah of
the future: the succah made from the skin of the Leviathan, and
(because of its luxuriousness) the succah of Sodom.[30]

THREE TYPES OF SUCCAH

There are, then, three types of succah. This has been made
explicit by Rabbi Ephraim Solomon ben Aaron of Luntshits
(1550–1619). According to him there is "the succah of Egypt, the
present succah [i.e., the succah of the generations], and the
future succah."[31] According to R. Ephraim Solomon, the succah
of Egypt (i.e., of the wilderness) and the present succah (i.e.,
of each generation) are incomplete. The succah of the future will
be complete because God's sovereignty will be one over the
world. In explaining what this means he refers to the rise of
manichean dualism, and indicates that the sovereignty of the
One is not yet accepted by all.

That there are three different types of succah means that the
succah is not an oneiric house nor a cosmological hut but a
historic hut. A classic Jewish work goes so far as to say, "Because
they make a succah and are exiled from house to succah, the
Holy One, Blessed be He, considers that as if they were exiled
to Babylonia."[32] The succah of the generations, the contemporary
succah, embodies historic events.

OTHER INTERPRETATIONS

There have been other interpretations of the succah. Nine-
teenth- and twentieth-century liberal Jews stressed the succah

as harvest hut. This view is untenable; for if the evolutionary interpretation of the development of the festival is correct, then liberal Judaism's celebration is a retrogression to pre-Mosaic celebration, a reentry to the pagan world's agricultural life, which is a dehistoricizing of the world.

Medieval Jewish philosophers and kabbalists stressed a kind of moralistic message of the succah: life is fragile and temporary. To know this, one leaves one's house, which appears enduring, and lives in the succah, which is fragile. This has become a commonly accepted cliché. It is not only highly individualistic but also embodies a dehistoricizing of the world.

The succah is neither agricultural space nor moralistic space. Neither is it dream space nor cosmological space. The succah is historic space. Dwelling in it is not a return to the wilderness, for to try to relive the desert experience would deny history, the life of the subsequent generations. The contemporary succah, the succah of each generation, points to the historic event of the Exodus from Egypt and the conquest of the Land of Israel. The contemporary succah points to the original event because of the original event's impact on the future generations.

But the contemporary succah also points to the future succah. When one leaves the succah one recites the following: "May it be Thy will, O Lord our God and God of our fathers, that as I have established and dwelt in this succah so may I have the merit in the coming year to dwell in the succah [made] of the skin of the Leviathan."[33] The succah of the generations points toward the future.

TIME AND PLACE ARE ONE

In recent years we have learned how important time is in Jewish tradition. The problem of space has troubled us. In our experience of exile and in our nineteenth-century concern for universalism, as opposed as these two realities are, we have rejected the local as parochial and provincial. Yet every culture presupposes an orientation in space in its encounter with the world. As we in our time have again learned how central history is for Jewish existence we must now recover the reality of space. No less a thinker than the Maharal of Prague (d. 1609) pointed out that time and place are one.[34] For Jewish existence time is not devalued as temporal and the world is not deprecated as mundane. Jewish holidays structure Jewish existence in the world where relationship between God and the covenantal People takes place.

Chapter 7

TEFILLAT GESHEM

THE JEWISH PRAYER FOR RAIN

THE PRAYER FOR RAIN, *Tefillat Geshem*, is recited on Shemini Azeret, the holiday of solemn assembly celebrated the day after Succot. This prayer, inserted at the repetition of the *musaf Amidah*, was composed by Elazar Ha-Kalir. It is an alphabetic acrostic of six stanzas, each of which begins with the word "Remember." God is asked to remember six personalities for whose merit He should give rain: Abraham, Isaac, Jacob, Moses, Aaron, and the Twelve Tribes. The Tribes, not individually named, are explicitly referred to. The others are referred to obliquely.

The Abraham stanza begins with *Ab* (father). The Isaac stanza's second line, "Thou didst tell . . . ," uses *sachta*, a subtle play on Isaac. The Jacob stanza hints at Jacob by means of a pun with letter reversal: *neavak*, a kind of paronomastic metathesis. The Moses stanza's "drawn-forth" puns on Moshe. The Aaron stanza and the Tribes stanza do not hint at names.

Despite the oblique references, this *Geshem* prayer is immediately understandable. Compact and rather brief, it contains no neologisms and practically no recondite allusions. *Geshem* is a prayer for rain, not in the country in which it is recited, but in the Land of Israel. Kalir, about whom practically nothing is known, lived in the diaspora a thousand or more years ago and may very well have never even visited the Land of Israel. Like Kalir, the vast majority of Jews who recited this prayer through the centuries were also diaspora Jews. That Kalir's *Geshem* became the prayer for rain was not accidental. It is an authentic expression of Jewish piety.

THE HUMAN CONCERN FOR RAIN

Rainmaking has always been a human concern. Travelers and anthropologists have reported on rainmaking ceremonies in various cultures. Zuni rainmaking, for example, was a complex, carefully structured ceremonial enterprise; its description takes up twenty-five closely printed pages.[1] Much simpler were the aboriginal Australian rainmaking rituals. The Dieri tribesmen informed their "spiritual ancestors who made and inhabited the earth in the dream-time prior to man . . . and [who] now live in the sky,"[2] that rain was needed. Then a trench was dug, over which was built a "large conical hut . . . covered with boughs,"[3] and the medicine men "pierce their arms to allow the blood to drop [symbolizing rain] on the old men [who] butt down the hut . . . to symbolize rain."[4] The Arunta tribe also constructed a similar hut in which magical songs were sung under the direction of a leader decorated with colored bands representing the rainbow.[5] In some tribes the one who performed the ritual went to a pool, sang to the water, and then sprinkled water in various directions.[6] In others, an arched bundle of grass, imitating a rainbow, was placed over a snake; and songs were sung in order to bring rain.[7]

A NONINDIGENOUS PRAYER

All aboriginal rainmaking rituals are rituals of autochthonous, or indigenous, tribes. The *Geshem* prayer, however, was neither composed nor recited by autochthonous people. Indeed its very references are primarily nonautochthonous. Abraham was not a native of the Land of Israel. Moses and Aaron never entered the Land. The tribes that crossed the Reed Sea (this is the reference to them in the prayer) were the generation that never entered the Land. Isaac and Jacob are the only autochthonous persons in the prayer; and the Jacob paragraph mentions only his experiences outside of the Land.

This is most significant. Autochthonous prayers and techniques are biologically oriented. *Tefillat Geshem*, overwhelmingly nonautochthonous, is historically oriented. The Dieri tribe called upon its ancestors who inhabited the earth in dream time, i.e., nonhistoric time. The personalities of the *Geshem* prayer, however, lived in historic time.

So, too, the aboriginal hut in contrast to the succah. The two structures are the opposite of each other. Aboriginal hut and arched bundle of grass stalks are rainmaking devices. The succah is a history hut, that the generations may "know" that God took them out of Egypt (Lev. 23:43).

A METAPHOR FOR FOES AND MARTYRS' BLOOD

The six references in the *Geshem* prayer are to those who lived in past history in a crisis situation. But the prayer also includes a sense of the present time. The last two lines, written most sparingly—only ten words in Hebrew—sum up the present exilic crisis: "For thy sake was the blood of their descendants spilt like water. Turn to us for our life is surrounded by foes like water."[8]

The culmination of this prayer is unexpected yet befits the basic orientation of the prayer. We noted that the historic personalities referred to were not native to the Land with the exceptions of Isaac and Jacob, the latter absent from the Land for twenty years, and that Moses, Aaron, and the tribes that crossed the Reed Sea never entered the Land. The culmination of the prayer, therefore, also embodies the historical-exilic rather than the biological-autochthonous: "the blood of the descendants spilt like water." Water is, here, a metaphor for the blood of the martyred descendants.

The past generations of the prayer, i.e., the ancestors and their descendants, lead into "us for our life is surrounded by foes like water." In this clause, water is a metaphor for the many enemies. That water can be a metaphor for both blood and foes presents no problem. For water, throughout this prayer, is interpreted historically and therefore multilaterally rather than biologically, which is unilateral.

THE PRAYER'S FLOW

There are significant absences from the prayer. The word *geshem* (rain) occurs only twice, in the brief introductory paragraphs, *Af Bri* and *Yatriah L'faleg*. In the core of the prayer *geshem* does not appear. Only *mayim* (water) is used; and it occurs thirty times. Water, we suggest, is more associated with historic persons than rain.

NO RAINMAKERS MENTIONED

Kalir had other possibilities that he must have intentionally avoided. Elijah and Jeremiah had been involved with rain, but with the denial of it. There are, as a matter of fact, no biblical rainmakers. However, there was one Jewish rainmaker, and he is absent from *Tefillat Geshem:* Honi, the so-called circle drawer. Kalir, who certainly knew the rabbinic texts that refer to Honi, must have intentionally avoided any reference to him.

It was not that there was the aspect of the magician about Honi. Moderns tend to make much of Honi's circle, assuming that the circle is a magical figure. This was not necessarily Kalir's view. For it is not certain that Honi drew a circle. He may have "dug a pit."[9] If he did, however, draw a circle around himself, he was neither necessarily nor regularly a "circle-drawer." *Hame'aggel* may refer to Honi's place of origin or may indicate that he repaired roofs or ovens;[10] and when asked to pray for rain, he drew a circle, or dug a pit, in which he stood, because, according to a modern scholar, Honi "imposed upon himself the restraint of having to remain within the circle for an indefinite period."[11]

There was reason for this self-imposed restraint. Having previously been asked to pray for rain and having too readily accepted, he was reproved by God "for his immodest demeanor" in that his earlier prayer was not answered.[12] That is why Honi subsequently stood within a circle or pit: "he binds himself firmly to his undertaking."[13]

The rabbinic tradition, the only source of information about Honi, had reservations about him. Simon ben Shetah wanted to put him in ban, considering him a sinner by virtue of his presumptuousness, but did not do so because God granted Honi's request, the request of a sinful but pampered son.[14]

The Jewish tradition has no office of rainmaker, and Honi's absence from the *Geshem* prayer is not accidental. Kalir rightly omitted him.

SIX CORE STANZAS AND PERSONS

The *Geshem* prayer is a carefully constructed composition. Its inclusions are as significant as its omissions. Geographic orientation is omitted. There are no references to east, west, south, or north. Included in the six core stanzas, however, are movements. The first and last stanzas (Abraham and the Tribes) embody linear movements. The third (Jacob) is also linear with, perhaps, a semicircular movement of Jacob's "rolling" a stone from off the well, a well significantly outside the Land. The second and fifth stanzas (Isaac and Aaron) have downward movements. The fourth stanza (Moses) has both downward and linear movements.

None of these movements is circular, and they are thus not the circles of nature, the realm of eternal recurrence. The emphasis on the linear is an aspect of the historical orientation of the prayer.

COMMUNITY AS SEVENTH PERSON

With its emphasis on the historical, the *Geshem* prayer is finely attuned to Jewish piety. That God is called upon to remember the six for whose merit He should give rain presupposes the faithful community outside of the Land, who remember the Land and its need of rain. That is the merit of the seventh personality, unmentioned in the prayer because it does the praying. The community's faithful memory makes it possible that its tongue not cleave to its palate as it prays for rain.

Chapter 8

THE PRIESTLY BLESSING

A PRAYER CONCERNING DREAMS

IN TRADITIONAL SYNAGOGUES during the holidays, the priests bless the congregation with the Priestly Blessing.[1] Blessing the congregation is a divinely ordained function, and the words used, according to the tradition, are divinely ordained.

During the course of the Priestly Blessing the congregation twice recites a prayer concerning dreams. Declaring "I am Thine and my dreams are Thine," each congregant continues: "I have dreamed a dream and I do not know what it is."[2] The person is troubled by the enigmatic quality of this dream. The congregant expresses the hope that it be God's will that all dreams be for personal and all Israel's good.

If the dreams that the person dreams are good dreams, he or she asks that they be strengthened and be made firm and fulfilled like the dreams of Joseph. But if the dreams need healing, the supplicant asks God to heal them as God healed King Hezekiah's sickness, Miriam's leprosy, and Naaman's leprosy. The prayer then refers to the bitter waters of Marah and Jericho changed by Moses and Elisha into sweet waters, although "change" and "sweet" are not used, since, presumably, "healing" is also applied to the waters.

The prayer concludes with the congregant asking God to "overturn all my dreams and those of all Israel unto the good" as God had "overturned the curse of Balaam so that it became a blessing."

JEWISH DREAM INTERPRETATION

This prayer is recited during the Priestly Blessing because of a suggestion made in the Talmud,[3] although the Talmud does not explain why that is the proper time for this prayer concerning dreams.

Dream interpretation has been important in Jewish historic existence. The biblical and rabbinic material on dreams is rather well known. Dream interpretation was also important in the medieval period as evinced by such works as the *Book of the Devout, Responsa from Heaven*, and the late *Interpretation of Dreams* by Solomon Almoli. The traditional Jewish view of dreams is complex. The belief that dreams are a kind of revelation was counterbalanced by the oft-quoted passage from Eccles. 5:3: "For a dream cometh through a multitude of business." But also important was a rabbinic assumption that the meaning of the dream is determined by the interpreter.[4] These three assumptions—that dreams may be revelations, may be nonsense, and are determined by the interpreter—serve to establish a sense of the ambiguity of dreams. That is why there is a prayer about dreams.

A PORTENT OF EVIL

Because a dream may be a portent of evil, the congregant asks for God's healing. The prayer refers to three instances of sickness: King Hezekiah's, Miriam's, and Naaman's.[5] Each, in some way, was healed by God. As God cures sickness so He is asked to "cure" dreams.

To these three instances of divine healing are added two other examples that subtly redefine the situation. Moses and Elisha had each changed bitter water into sweet water.[6] They did not transform a liquid into a solid but only modified the quality of the water. That is why these two examples are cited in the prayer. The congregant asks not for a different dream but that the dream be modified, that its character be changed.

The climax of the prayer refers to Balaam, whose intention to curse Israel had been overturned, by God, into a blessing. The congregant beseeches God: "So mayest thou overturn all my dreams for myself and all Israel unto the good."

SEVEN HISTORICAL LEADERS

Why were these seven examples chosen and others excluded? Each of these seven was, in some way, a community leader. Joseph was "lord of all Egypt" (Gen. 45:9); Hezekiah was king of Judah (2 Kings 18); Miriam as prophetess (Exod. 15:20) was a leader; Naaman, a pious pagan, was a military commander and "a great man with his master" (2 Kings 5:1); Moses and Elisha were community leaders. Balaam, a gentile prophet, was a sort of political leader since he was hired to deal with the invading Israelites (Num. 22:6).

The dream prayer associates the congregant's dream with the lives of historic persons who acted in the everyday world. This is significant because in dreaming "the temporal order disintegrates" and "the dreamer is alone in his dream world."[7] Since the dreamer is alone in a situation of temporal disorder—modalities untenable for Jewish existence, which is historic and covenantal—the congregant praying for healing associates his situation with historic persons in covenantal situations. The congregant hopes to transcend the temporal disorder and solipsistic existence that are the ambiguities of dreams.

DREAMS AS OPTICAL

We know from personal experience that dreams are for the most part optical experiences rather than auditory. The Hebrew word for dream, *halom,* is a sight term.[8] In contrast to the optic, "acoustic impressions which require the sequence of time to form a whole cannot, as fragmentary presences, be used by the dreamer to make up an encompassing meaningful unity."[9] This accounts for a curious but significant aspect of the Priestly Blessing: according to the tradition, one must not look at the priests during the Blessing. Many reasons are given for this. We suggest the following.

Since dream impressions are for the most part optical and temporally disordered, but "sound has process character" is temporally ordered, "and gives only dynamic and never static character . . . , discloses . . . not an object but a dynamical event at the locus of sound,"[10] the Priestly Blessing rejects the optic and is of necessity acoustic. For what is disclosed during the Blessing is not a static object but the dynamical event of blessing in the everyday world. From the standpoint of the tradition, God, not the priests, blesses the congregation. And God is never object.

THE BLESSING AS HEALING

The Blessing is a dynamical event at the locus of the sound. Significantly, this blessing of the congregation is traditionally referred to as the Raising of the Hands.

THE BLESSING AS ACOUSTIC

The Blessing, as we have said, is acoustic and therefore embodies temporal sequence. After the precentor exclaims "Priests" and the congregation joins with three words of proclamation, the priests recite a benediction that concludes with "and commanded us to bless Thy people with love." Here, and in what follows, there is time sequence.

> FIRST: The precentor exclaims and the priests chant the first three words of the blessing.
>
> SECOND: The congregants recite the prayer concerning dreams, while the priests chant a melody and conclude with the third word.
>
> THIRD: The precentor exclaims and the priests chant the next five words.

FOURTH: The dream prayer is recited again, the priests chanting and concluding the second group of words.

FIFTH: The precentor exclaims and the priests chant the concluding words of the Blessing.

SIXTH: The congregation and the priests each recite a prayer in which blessings are asked for "My people Israel" and the Land of Israel.

In this dynamic event that rejects the optical, what would the congregants see if they looked? The priests stand shoeless on the platform, initially with backs toward the congregation; next, facing the congregation, the priests raise their hands and arrange their fingers a certain way. At five different times during the Blessing they face south and north.

But none of this is seen, for "objectivity emerges preeminently from sight . . . the sense of the passive observer par excellence."[11] The congregants, however, are not passive observers but are in an existential situation of intersubjectivity: God, the priests, and the congregation responding to each other.

THE BLESSING AS POWER, PEACE, AND LOVE

In what sense is the Priestly Blessing a therapy? First, none of the classical Hebrew terms for dream interpretation occur in the Blessing or in the prayer concerning dreams. The basic terms are "healing" and "turning over" (or "turning around").

Second, and more important, is the conception of blessing. It is during the Blessing that the prayer about dreams is recited. This blessing is formulated in Jewish scripture, and there is a scriptural conception of blessing. A blessing is "the vital power, without which no living being can exist . . . Blessing is life power . . . the power to live in its deepest and most comprehensive sense."[12] Wisdom is involved with blessing, for both are "the power to work and succeed."[13] So, too, understanding, which is "the power to live and accomplish the purpose one has set in life."[14]

This biblical conception of blessing fits the conception of therapy as formulated by a modern student of psychology: "The therapeutic purpose involves increasing the patient's knowledge and his capacity for effective life decisions."[15] So, too, the Blessing gives power and strength, vigor, wisdom, and understanding in order that one can live, work, and achieve one's goals.

If one lacks the blessing, one lacks peace; for peace and blessing are the same.[16] That is why the first word in the Priestly Blessing is "bless" and the last word is "peace." Significantly, the last (Hebrew) word of the meditation verse that accompanies the priestly "Shalom" is "I will heal him" (Isa. 57:19); and "Shalom" is the last word of the congregation's concluding prayer.

In Jewish scripture, the source of the Priestly Blessing, "Love . . . is identical with peace itself."[17] It is not accidental, therefore, that the introductory benediction recited by the priests concludes with "love," the last word of the Blessing is "peace," and the last word of the congregation's prayer is "peace." As blessing and peace may be identified, so, too, in the tradition, love is included in peace.

The wisdom and understanding, together with the power, peace, and love that the Blessing gives, make up not a theoretical knowledge but an existential knowledge. The congregant, as we have noted, does not ask for the interpretation of this dream but for its healing. For interpretation of dreams, according to the tradition, one goes to a dream interpreter. For healing one stands before the priests during the priestly Raising of the Hands. The words of Frieda Fromm-Reichmann can serve as a gloss to the controlling premise of the Priestly Blessing: "The patient needs an experience, not an explanation."[18]

Chapter 9

THE NINTH OF AV

THE SORROWS OF EXILE

TISHAH B'AV, the ninth of Av, commemorates a series of major defeats in Jewish historic existence, particularly the destruction of the First and Second Temples. Other fasts commemorate other troubles: the seventeenth of Tammuz, the breach of the walls of First-Temple Jerusalem; the tenth of Tevet, the siege of Jerusalem by Nebuchadnezzar; the third of Tishri, the assassination of Gedaliah; the thirteenth of Adar, the fast of Esther.

FAST COMMEMORATING DEFEAT

Of the fasts commemorating defeats, the Ninth of Av is the most important, beginning the previous evening and climaxing a three-week period of sorrow. Mourning, fasting, not wearing leather shoes, not washing oneself, refraining from sexual intercourse, not greeting others, abstaining from the pleasure of

85

studying Torah, uncomfortable seating, reciting lamentations—these constitute Tishah B'Av.

A LACK OF NOURISHMENT

Nourishment is prohibited not because of asceticism, but because nourishment makes life possible and in defeat shortage of food is destructive of life. Throughout the Book of Lamentations and the rest of the liturgy of the Ninth of Av, references are made to hunger. So desperate for food were the people at the First Temple's destruction that mothers cooked their children, according to Lamentations. A millennium and a half later, the great liturgical poet Kalir, whose compositions make up a large part of the day's liturgy, composed the elegy, "When I [think how] women could devour their own offspring . . . Woe is me,"[1] an indication that hunger is one of the basic themes of the day.

CRYING AND WEEPING

Together with hunger, another theme in the texts and in those who recite them is crying. Early in Lamentations, the second verse, reference is made to Jerusalem's crying and to her tears. The liturgy contains references to weeping throughout.

The Ninth of Av commemorates not only the destruction of the two Temples but also the destruction of the Land of Israel. This is expressed in many ways. Solomon Ibn Gabriol's "Samaria Lifts Up Her Voice," a dialogue between Samaria and Jerusalem that has been incorporated into the service, is a lament on the destruction of the whole country.

A LAMENT FOR ALL PEOPLE OF ISRAEL

The liturgy of the day expresses a concern for the People of Israel wherever they may be. Menachem ben Machir's eleventh-century elegy, "I raise my lament,"[2] refers explicitly to the crusaders killing Jews in 1096. Joseph of Chartre's twelfth-century composition, "O, God, other lords beside Thee have ruled over us,"[3] is an elegy for the martyrs of York. Kalonymous ben Judah's eleventh-century elegy is for the martyrs of Speyer, Worms, and Mayence.[4]

EVERY JEW IS IN EXILE

Nowhere in the liturgy of the day is there a statement that in every generation a Jew is obliged to see himself as if he were expelled from the Land of Israel. There is no necessity for an *as if*. It is patent to every Jew that he is in Exile. God, however, is to be reminded of the exilic situation. In Kalir's composition for the day, "How in Thy Wrath Thou Didst Hasten to Destroy," it is stated eleven times that God did not remember various things, and eleven times God is urged to remember "what has befallen us."[5] In "Thou Didst Say, 'I Will Surely Do You Good,'"[6] God is questioned as to why defeats occurred and is reminded of His promises, as He is reminded of the situation in the composition, "Remember What the Enemy Has Done in the Temple."[7]

A LITURGICAL NONMEAL

The observance of the Ninth of Av takes place primarily in the synagogue. The participants, seated on the floor or on low stools, are poorly dressed; they recite the lamentations and weep. As the Passover Seder is a liturgical meal, the Ninth of Av service is a liturgical nonmeal. Throughout the liturgy the emphasis, as we have noted, is on hunger, something not mentioned in the liturgy of Yom Kippur, an equally rigorous fast day. The Exodus from Egypt and the Passover Seder stand in the background of the Ninth of Av liturgical nonmeal service. Commemorating the great defeats, the Ninth of Av presupposes, because it contradicts, the great redemption from Egypt.

EXODUS AND EXILE CONTRASTED

The liturgy consciously calls attention to the Exodus. Together with tangential references to Passover—e.g., "they who partook of the paschal lamb on Passover's vigil"[8]—lengthy references to the Exodus are made. The meditation *Esh Tukad B'Api* contrasts Exile with Exodus: "The fire [of joy] is kindled within, as I think [of the time] when I departed from Egypt . . . I will raise lamentations, as I recall [the time] when I departed from Jerusalem."[9] The contrast is drawn twenty times.

Exodus and Exile are contrasted in a number of compositions recited on the Ninth of Av. Ephraim ben Jacob's twelfth-century composition *Az Amarti* makes the contrast.[10] The remarkably learned Kalir surely knew that the day of the week on which the first day of Passover falls is the day on which Tishah B'Av falls, and this may have been on his mind when he composed the elegy "On This Night My Children Weep and Wail, on the Night My Temple was Destroyed."[11]

Compositions in other Jewish liturgical traditions of the Ninth of Av make the Exodus-Exile contrast. One, "Why is this night [of the Ninth of Av] different from all the nights of the year,"[12] repeated six times, calls the Seder to mind; another, "Why is this day different from all [other days] of the year,"[13] contrasts the sorrows of the day with the joys of Passover.

The liturgical situation in the synagogue also makes the contrast. The home seder is a freeman's banquet: reclining, eating, drinking wine, singing praises. At the Ninth of Av's liturgical nonmeal one sits uncomfortably, festival clothing is not worn, hallelujah songs are not sung.

THE POLARITIES OF JEWISH EXISTENCE

The festival of Passover and the fast of Tishah B'Av embody the two polarities of Jewish existence: Exodus and Exile. Jewish piety, affirming that Jewish existence has meaning, is rooted in the Exodus from Egypt. The tradition from its very beginning points to the Promised Land; and the Exodus from Egypt was undertaken to reach the Land. But Exile contradicts and thereby denies Exodus.

A modern philosopher, Karl Lowith, has pointed out, "There is only one very particular history—that of the Jews—that as a political history can be interpreted strictly religiously . . . The Jewish prophets . . . had . . . an unshakable faith in God's providential purpose for His chosen people, punishing and rewarding them for disobedience and obedience."[14] Lowith reflects further on this statement: "Most amazing, the strength of this faith in a divine moral purpose in history rose to a climax just when all empirical evidence was *against* it [his emphasis] . . . The prophets saw in the ruin of Israel not a proof of the powerlessness . . . [of God] but an indirect manifestation of His universal power."[15]

Both Passover and Tishah B'Av testify to God's universal power. Together they represent not contradiction but paradox. We have noted that the Tishah B'Av liturgy refers to Exodus and Passover. It should be noted, too, that the Passover Haggadah also refers to Exile. Its statement "Thou wilt pursue them in anger and destroy them [the nations] from under the Heavens of the Lord" is a quotation from the Book of Lamentations;[16] and the concluding expression of hope, "Next year in Jerusalem" is an exilic statement. Indeed, the very celebration of Passover is itself a paradox; for Passover, testifying to God's power that freed the Jews from Egyptian servitude, has been consistently celebrated during the Jews' longest Exile, *Galut Edom*.

REMEMBERING JERUSALEM

Once each year Jews remember two gentile cities. On Yom Kippur Jews remember Nineveh, the city that repented in response to Jonah's prophesying. A few Sabbaths later, Jews remember Babel, the city that God obliterated because of its sinful pride. On Tishah B'Av, however, the Jew cries for Jerusalem, the one city that the Jew has promised never to forget and that he calls on God to remember. It has been said that "in crying out, we experience our power or our infirmity."[17] On the Ninth of Av when Jews cry we experience both our infirmity and our power. Our infirmity, for life in exile is fragile as twenty centuries of exile demonstrate; our power, for we are strong enough to remember Jerusalem and strong enough to endure the Exodus-Exile paradox.

WEEPING'S EFFECTS

What is achieved by crying on this fast day? The phenomenon of crying has not received much attention by thinkers despite the fact that crying is "one of the most striking peculiarities of human nature . . . that distinguishes man from the animals."[18] Schopenhauer argued that "we never weep directly over the pain that is felt, but always over its repetition in reflection."[19] Schopenhauer concluded that "we then find our own state . . . deserving of sympathy . . . [so that] we ourselves are most in need of help . . . Accordingly, *weeping is sympathy with ourselves* . . ."[20] He uses an anecdote to clarify this self-sympathy that comes from crying after reflecting on pain: "A client, after listening to the presentation of his case in court by his counsel, burst into tears and exclaimed, 'I never thought I had suffered half so much till I listened to it here today.' "[21] According to Schopenhauer, there is a double movement here: "We feel that we endure more than we could see another endure . . . and in this peculiarly involved frame of mind, . . . the directly felt suffering comes to perception only in a doubly indirect way, pictured as the suffering of another and sympathized with as such, and then suddenly [it is] perceived again as our own . . ."[22]

REPETITION IN REFLECTION

Schopenhauer's analysis enables us to understand weeping on the Ninth of Av. Our weeping over Jerusalem and all the other destroyed Jewish communities is a crying not over immediate pain but over its "repetition in reflection." We weep over "their" felt pain, and since we in our particular times are in exile, our "weeping is sympathy with ourselves." It is with the recitation of the lamentation texts of the day that we burst into tears, for we did not realize that we had suffered so much until we listen to it on this day. The suffering of the others, suddenly perceived as our own, makes us cry on Tishah B'Av. In this situation, as Schopenhauer indicated, we find that "we ourselves are most in need of help." We therefore call on God to remember us, as we remember Jerusalem and all the other communities.

Schopenhauer notes that "people who are either hard-hearted or without imagination do not readily weep; indeed weeping is always regarded as a sign of a certain degree of goodness of character and it disarms anger."[23] Our crying is a sign that we are not the stiff-necked, hard-hearted people in relationship to

God that we were before exile, but that we embody a certain degree of goodness of character that will perhaps disarm God's anger.

LAUGHTER AND TEARS

The approach to the problematics of the Exodus-Exile paradox is dual: tears and laughter. Purim laughs at Exile. On Purim Jews adopt the comic role, dressing as gentiles, as transvestites, cursing Mordecai and blessing Haman. The comic is a response to incongruity; on Purim the incongruity between Exodus and Exile. Purim celebrants are most conscious of Exile. The Scroll of Esther depicts a Jewish community in Exile. Two verses in the Scroll[24] are chanted to the tune of the book of Lamentations. Exile is thereby played-out in comedy on Purim.

Tishah B'Av, on the other hand, weeps at Exile. On Purim God's presence hovers in the background; in the Scroll of Esther no one speaks to or about God because God does not adopt the comic role. On Tishah B'Av God is constantly addressed; Exile is called to His attention. Tishah B'Av, in its own particular way, is a statement of Jewish faith in a divine moral purpose in history and a witnessing to God's universal power.

Chapter 10

PURIM

THE CELEBRATION OF DISORDER

PURIM IS THE strangest holiday. Its name is not Jewish, but refers
to the lottery cast by the enemy of the Jews. Only this holiday
features the reading of a strange scroll, done in a strange fashion.
It permits the making of noise, the eruption of disorder at specific
points in the reading, yet one must not miss a single word.

STRANGE JEWISH CHARACTERS

The Scroll of Esther is an exotic work. Its Jewish characters are
strange. The heroine has two names. Esther, most frequently
used, is probably not Hebrew. One talmudic sage interprets it,
"The gentile nations called her 'Ist 'har.' "[1] Her Jewish name was
Hadassah. Yet, the scroll is called the Scroll of Esther, not Hadassah.

So, too, the name Mordecai: moderns have argued that the name Mordecai is not Hebrew. The sages also betray uncertainty. They were of the opinion that he had another name, obviously Hebraic: Petahya.

Esther and Mordecai, each having two names, are diaspora Jews: one name in the gentile world, another in the Jewish world. They are hyphenated Jews. Furthermore, they are not married. Ahasuerus, the gentile king, is married. Haman is married and has children. Esther is without parents and without Jewish husband although she is an adult. Mordecai, too, is not a family man. This is not the traditional Jewish situation.

AN ASSIMILATED COMMUNITY

Other strange elements in the scroll are heard. The Jewish community is an assimilated one. Esther enters a beauty contest and marries the gentile king without telling him of her Jewishness—an act that has made Jews uncomfortable. Indeed, kabbalists were so driven to resolve this issue that they maintained that Ahasuerus actually slept with a phantom resembling Esther.

Mordecai's Jewishness is also somewhat marginal. Traditional commentators make the pointed observation that he should have spent more time in the yeshivah and less time at the royal court.

What a luxurious life these Jews lived. They no longer had the ideal of the land of milk and honey, the pastoral ideal of the Land of Israel. Eretz Yisrael is never mentioned; only a brief reference to the exile "from Jerusalem."

We encounter a gentile world in the scroll. Even the vocabulary of the book is full of Persian words. In this gentile world an immense amount of drinking takes place. The word *Mishteh*, drinking party or bash, occurs as many times as it does in the rest of the Bible. Many parties are mentioned in the book.

These Jews are highly assimilated. They live outlandish lives. They are so assimilated that at first one hardly senses a Jewish community; it is absent from most of the scroll. One encounters two Jews involved with the royal court. The members of the Jewish community must each have pursued an individual career.

Just as the Land of Israel is missing from the scroll, just as the Community of Covenantal Israel is largely missing, so is God absent from the Book of Esther. The proper name is not found in the book; nor does *Elohim* occur. It has been suggested that *YHVH* is missing because the writer did not want to refer to God by name since the environment was contaminated: drunkenness, beauty contests, assimilation.

A ZEALOUS BUT LOYAL COMMUNITY

For all its assimilation, however, this Jewish community was a zealous one, fully aware of itself and, ultimately, authentic. The same Mordecai who had instructed Esther not to reveal her origins had revealed his Jewishness, which was at the root of his refusal to bow down to Haman. Furthermore, he was not an isolated, highly individualized Jew but a member of a recognizable Jewish community.

We become aware of all this through Haman's eyes. Haman saw Mordecai not as a career man at court who happened to be Jewish but as a member of the Jewish community: "It seemed contemptible in his eyes to lay hands on Mordecai alone; for they had made known to him the people of Mordecai; wherefore Haman sought to destroy all the Jews that were throughout the whole kingdom of Ahasuerus, even the people of Mordecai."[2]

Through Haman's eyes we also see the community. "There is a certain people scattered abroad and dispersed among the peoples in all the provinces . . . their laws are diverse from those of every people; neither keep they the king's laws . . ."[3] The words are a perversion of reality. The Jews were loyal. Esther had obediently become the king's wife; Mordecai had warned the king of the plot to murder him; when it came to fighting for their lives the Jews obtained letters authorizing self-protection.

Their loyalty to the gentile state is indicated in another way. The first reference to Mordecai tells us that he "had been carried away from Jerusalem with the captives that had been carried away with Jeconiah, king of Judah, whom Nebuchadnezzar the king of Babylon had carried away."[4] It had been these people who had received a letter from the prophet Jeremiah telling them, in God's name, to "seek the peace of the city whither I have caused you to be carried away captive, and pray to the Lord for it; for in the peace thereof shall ye have peace."[5] There is no reason to assume that the advice was rejected.

So Haman's words to the king were a perverse reading of Jewish reality. What was true, however, was that the Jews were recognizable as a distinct group. The Jews depicted in the Book of Esther are exilic Jews; they do many non-Jewish things, yet they remain fundamentally Jewish.

STRANGE TENSIONS AND REVERSALS

Not only are Mordecai and Esther rather strange in terms of their Jewishness, not only is the Jewish community rather strange, but everything about the book is strange. For example, the word for "law," *dt*, occurs twenty times, ten times as much as in all the rest of Scripture; yet much lawlessness is noted. The king's anger is stirred up against Vashti; he easily permits Haman to destroy the Jews; without much persuasion he permits the Jews to attack their enemies.

Other amazing reversals are noted in the book aside from the king's reversal about the Jews. Vashti was rejected because modesty had prevented her from attending the noblemen's party. Yet Esther was made queen partly because of her winning modesty. Initially, after Vashti's refusal, the princes had advised the king, "this deed of the queen will come abroad unto all the women to make their husbands contemptible in their eyes," suggesting Vashti's removal so that "all the wives will give to their husbands honor . . . that every man should bear rule in his own house, and speak according to the language of his own people."[6] On the one hand a fear is expressed of women ruling over men, yet women do rule over men: Mordecai turns to Esther for help; Haman goes to his wife for advice; Esther maneuvers so that the king destroys Haman.

The king is not the ruler. He is governed by wine, women, and upstarts. He keeps reversing himself. He is a topsy-turvy king.[7]

REVERSALS OF IDENTITY

Jewish tradition has long been aware of the curious, topsy-turvy quality of the Scroll of Esther. One old tradition asserts that Haman was a slave of Mordecai. Mordecai had supplied a starving Haman with food during a military campaign. For this food Haman had sold himself to Mordecai. A late traditional commentary adds, "Accordingly, Haman became a 'Canaanite slave,' circumcised, and therefore, obliged to fulfill the commandments that a [Jewish] woman is responsible for. If so, indeed Haman is called a Jew, for the word *Jew* is a generic term [for one who rejects idolatry]."[8]

As bizarre as that may appear to us, the Jewish masses understood both the scroll and the festival of Purim as being topsy-turvy. They expressed it sharply: Purim is known as the holiday when Jews become *goyim* and *goyim* become Jews. There is a truth to this folk observation. In the scroll, gentiles do become Jews;[9] and, as we have noted, Jews were assimilationists.

After initially being dressed in the king's robes, Mordecai is dressed this way a second time.[10] Change of clothing is significant, for clothing is one of the most intimate aspects of one's personality. Rooted in this is the tradition of wearing costumes and masks on Purim. One is permitted to dress up not only like Esther or Mordecai—that is, in the costume of the wife of a gentile king, or in that of a gentile king—one may dress as Haman as well. In the wearing of gentile clothing one becomes a gentile, if only for a little while. Some truth, therefore, can be given to the statement that Jews become *goyim* on Purim. It happens in the scroll; it happens on the festival.

REVERSALS OF GENDER ROLES

The change of clothing is involved with role reversal. Aside from gentile clothing, one is permitted to dress in the clothing of the opposite sex, something that is normally stringently forbidden. On Purim not only do Jews become gentiles, Jewish men can become women and Jewish women can become men. The Hasidic rebbe Abraham Joshua Heschel of Apta stated that Jews enjoyed this change of clothing. He wrote, "As we see in the days of Purim: when a man changes his garments and dresses in the garments of a woman, pleasure and joy result from this. Truly, the essence of pleasure comes about because of a change of a thing to its opposite."[11] This observation by a Hasidic thinker is also made in the twentieth century by a student of play, Roger Caillois, who says about changes of costume, "The pleasure lies in being different or in passing for another."[12] Role reversal makes for pleasure.

The wearing of gentile costumes on Purim is clearly rooted in the Scroll of Esther. This does not seem to be the case in donning clothing of the opposite sex. We believe, however, that it is an important aspect of the Purim celebration. To understand this we must reflect on biblical modes of thought. From the standpoint of the Bible,

> The drama of man under God cannot unfold without the continuous existence of the mankind that is supposed to live in accordance with the Instructions *(torot)*. Man, therefore, with the accent on his reproductive capacity, is the second major concern of the Israelite historians. Mankind is conceived as a clan deriving its community bond from a common ancestor. History, under this aspect, becomes an account of the generations *(toldot)*. The symbol of the *toldot* applies to the whole course of Israelite history.[13]

A startling exception to this is the Book of Esther. Medieval Jews were aware of this anomaly. *Sefer Hasidim*, the medieval Jewish book of the devout, reflected on this issue. Commenting on the opening phrase of Genesis 5,

> This is the book of the generations . . . a [biblical] book that is not concerned with the generations *[toldot]* of Israel, does not [therefore] contain the Divine name [YHVH]. For example, the *Scroll of Esther.* Because Ahasuerus, who was a gentile, took her to wife . . . and the book is about a gentile cohabiting with an Israelite woman, the [Divine] name is unknown to the *Scroll of Esther.*[14]

History, *toldot*, is missing from Esther.

That is why Jews in Eastern Europe, at least, donned the clothing of the opposite sex. They enacted thereby the denial of *toldot*; for Esther and Mordecai were without family. The man who wears woman's clothing and the woman who wears man's clothing exchange social and, by implication, biological roles, but incomplete biological roles. The man stops being a man; the woman stops being woman. There can be, therefore, no family.

The seriousness of this is obvious once we know, in the words of Erwin Straus, that "by means of the family the individual stands in relation to history."[15]

DRUNKENNESS, FOOD SNATCHING, AND HITTING

So, too, drunkenness: according to the tradition, "It is the duty of a man to mellow himself on Purim until he cannot tell the difference between 'cursed be Haman' and 'blessed be Mordecai.'"[16] As we have indicated, much drinking is related in the book, and drinking is urged in the tradition. That one will become tipsy, unable to tell the difference between blessing and cursing, is a part of the Purim festival rooted in the text.

Drunken people are disoriented; the world becomes topsy-turvy; they fall. It is not accidental that the verb "to fall" occurs quite a number of times in the scroll, for the drunken, falling man encounters the world as topsy-turvy, as disordered.

Another curious Purim custom is noteworthy. It seems to have been a custom in Eastern Europe to snatch food from one another and hit one another on Purim.[17] The legal codes are of the opinion that these actions do not constitute a violation of the prohibitions against stealing and assault. Strange as it may seem, these customs, too, are rooted in the scroll. They also serve to structure the holiday as topsy-turvy.

A CAREFULLY WRITTEN WORK

The Scroll of Esther is a carefully written work, hinting at more than it says explicitly. Of importance is Mordecai's genealogy. He is the son of Jair, the son of Kish, a Benjaminite. Haman's genealogy is also important. He is the son of Hammedatha, the Agagite. We are to remember that King Saul had been ordered by God, through Samuel, to destroy the Amalekites and all their possessions. Saul captured Agag, their king, spared him and all their best things.[18] Chapter nine of the Scroll of Esther says three times that when the Jews of Persia fought back, "on the spoil they laid not their hand."

Thus Mordecai is related to Saul, Haman to Agag. In the Saul-Agag conflict the Children of Israel did take of the spoil. In the

Mordecai-Haman conflict the Jews do not take of the spoil. But traditionally Jews not only dress in the clothing of the opposite sex, denying *toldot*, not only do they curse Mordecai and so deny their Jewishness, they also stretch forth their hands to the possessions of Jews. Purim is a topsy-turvy festival. Some people have even doubted that it was a festival; there is a Jewish folk expression that with its mockery gets at something true: Fever is no sickness; and Purim is no festival.[19]

PURIM AS PLAYING EXILE

Purim is play time in Jewish tradition. Such play serves an important function. Play has been studied by many thinkers down the ages. For our study, the words of Nietzsche serve to interpret the meaning of Purim as play time: "I know of no other way of coping with great tasks, than play."[20] This is what Purim accomplishes; it enables the Jew to cope with a great task: coming to grips with Exile.

One of the students of play in our time, the phenomenological philosopher Eugen Fink, discusses play and the player:

> Here we find a quite peculiar "schizophrenia," a kind of split personality that is not to be mistaken for a manifestation of mental illness. The player who participates in a game executes in the real world an action of a familiar type. Within the context of the internal meaning of play, however, he is taking over a role. Here we must distinguish between the real man who "plays" and the man created by the role within the play. The player hides his real self behind his role and is submerged in it. He lives *in* his role with a singular intensity, and yet not like the schizophrenic who is unable to distinguish between "reality" and "illusion." The player can recall himself from his role; while playing, man retains a knowledge of his double existence, however greatly reduced this knowledge may be. Man exists in two spheres simultaneously, not for lack of concentration or out of forgetfulness but because the double personality is essential to play.[21]

Purim is playing exile. Exile is a basic phenomenon of Jewish existence. It must be grasped existentially. Purim does that. It is the enacting of exile.

Eugen Fink was not thinking of Purim, but we who think of Purim are startled by his reference to a "quite peculiar 'schizophrenia,' a kind of split personality that is not to be mistaken for a manifestation of mental illness." This is so because the player of the role can distinguish between the real and the illusory, can recall himself from his role.

This is true of the Jew on Purim who dons the clothing of the opposite sex; who becomes mellow with drink and curses and blesses the wrong persons; who, in eating hamantaschen or dressing like him, assimilates something of Haman; who wears the gentile clothing of Mordecai or Esther.

While playing these roles, the Jew retains a knowledge of his double existence, a Jew in exile: a Mordecai-Petahya, an Esther-Hadassah. If "double personality is essential to play," Purim, rich in double personalities (even Haman can be interpreted as Mordecai's Jew), is, in essence, play.

A COMIC FRAME OF DISORDER AND MERRIMENT

Two basic elements make up Purim, disorder and merriment. They are intimately interrelated. The response to the disorder that is life in exile is merriment. It need not have been that way. The fast of Esther is a prelude to Purim, but it is not Purim. Fasts are serious, but Purim is fun time. Other possibilities also were present. Purim could have been a pleasant festival stressing the serious, somewhat like Shavuot. Yet Purim stresses the comic.

Rightly so. "The comic frame should enable people *to be observers of themselves, while acting. Its ultimate would not be passiveness* but *maximum consciousness.* One would transcend himself by noting his own foibles."[22]

This observation by Kenneth Burke, the literary critic, is suggestive partly of Fink's observation but goes further, for Burke also grapples with the problem of history. He writes, "The comic frame . . . might mitigate somewhat the difficulties in engineering a shift to new symbols of authority, as required by the new social relationships that the revolutions of historic environment have made necessary. It might provide important cues for the composition of one's life, which demands accommodation to the structure of others' lives."[23]

The Scroll of Esther depicts a Jewish community in exile, facing "difficulties in engineering a shift to new symbols of authority"; they no longer live in Eretz Yisrael; they no longer are an autonomous community. New social relationships are made necessary by a revolution of their historic environment. They must accommodate themselves to other—that is, gentile—lives.

So Purim's comic frame is important, but so is disorder. All the Purim activities that make for disorder are in essence deviations from the norm—at all other times prohibited, but sanctioned on Purim.

AN ANALOGY FROM "CAT HARBOUR"

Many social scientists have studied sanctioned deviations. Of particular interest for us is James Faris's study of a Newfoundland community, Cat Harbour.[24] It need hardly be said that twentieth-century Cat Harbour is as radically different a community from the community of covenantal Israel during the last twenty centuries as can be imagined. Nevertheless, from a study of Cat Harbour we can learn something about Purim.

In certain situations in Cat Harbour—"occasions," in their vocabulary—"it would appear that behavior pertaining at these occasions is topsy-turvy and totally different from what one might expect."[25] The occasions that interest us are the "Times," situations of "social 'license' often obtaining at weddings, Christmas parties and 'scoffs.' " A "time is a situation where the deviations and the role 'reversal' sanctioned by the occasion are fully achieved."[26] Otherwise, they are sins. So, too, is the Purim situation. The topsy-turvy things that Jews do on Purim are sanctioned by the occasion, otherwise they would be regarded as sins.

Drinking at Cat Harbour is of interest. "Men who otherwise seldom drink are often intoxicated at weddings, an expected and sanctioned deviation, a role reversal, as it were, from the rigidly temperant facade normally maintained."[27] This is why Purim drinking is important. It is an aspect of role reversal that leads to disorientation.

A characteristic of Christmastide in Cat Harbour are the Mummers, "the disguised individuals who go from house to house and who, in the disguise, often engage in activities considered a complete breach in normal circumstances."[28] Faris adds, the behavior which is regarded appropriate in these deviant circumstances, the behavior in which the Mummers engage is conceptually associated with strangers, from the representatives of the evil and potentially dangerous outside world."[29] This is true of Purim. The role reversal in Purim is associated with gentiles. Gentiles are drinkers; Mordecai and Esther wear gentile robes. Wearing the clothes of the opposite sex, Jews opt out of *toldot* and become *goyim*, strangers, representatives of the dangerous outside world.

A third "time" in Cat Harbour is the scoff, when a few married couples get together and have a party. Games are played; the men drink; there is sexual joking and license. The food for a scoff is "bucked," taken from someone else's garden or cellar. The sexual license of the scoff is not found in Purim. Yet the wearing of clothes of the opposite sex is a kind of promiscuity, a kind of confusion and mixture.[30] The common important element in the Cat Harbour scoff and Purim is the "bucking," which we have seen is a legitimate enterprise on Purim, although some of the pious were ill at ease with it.[31]

Faris sums up his analysis of "times" as follows: "In the role reversal of the 'times' people define their conception of what is 'reverse' by the most deviant category known to them, the symbols and beliefs and behavior they regard as characterizing the stranger."[32] We believe this is also true of Purim. The whole range of things that characterize Purim are aspects of the most deviant category the Jews know, namely the *goy*.

"Cat Harbour was originally settled in a harsh and demanding environment for pressing social reasons. These threatening circumstances gave rise to and helped reinforce a stereotype of the representative of the 'other world'; the potentially dangerous 'stranger,' the hostile outsider."[33] The Jewish exile environment, too, is harsh and demanding. The threatening historic situations did reinforce stereotypes of the dangerous stranger. Purim's role reversals, all of them, are the reversals of the hostile stranger.

PURIM IN THE DAYS OF THE MESSIAH

One tradition asserts that at the coming of the Messiah, all the holidays will be revoked. Only the days of Purim will remain in effect.[34] Many of the traditional commentators are baffled by this. In the technical sense, Purim is not a holiday. It is referred to as the "days of Purim." The traditional commentators found it strange that the festivals will be revoked but not Purim.

The tradition that Purim will not be revoked is rooted in a sure grasp of what Purim is. Indeed, the days of Purim are a necessity in the time of the Messiah. An observation of Elijah Ha-Cohen, author of the compendium *Midrash Talpiot*, will help us to understand the tradition of Purim's continuation: "Only in the days of the Messiah, after the wars have been settled, will the light of Torah begin to shine. Israel will then be secure, will recount the events of history, what happened to them in exile. [They will do this], so as to give praise and thanks to the Holy One, Blessed be He, for out of the dust heaps has He raised the poor."[35]

In the days of the Messiah, Israel will talk about what happened before peace was established, what happened in exile, the disorder in Jewish existence. In order to know existentially the new order in history, the order established by the Messiah, one must be aware of the disorder of former days, the topsy-turvy world of exile. Therefore, Purim will not pass away; the celebration of disorder will not be revoked. Only through the occasion of disorder can we *know* order.

Chapter 11

HANUKKAH

PURITY AND POLITICS IN HISTORY

HANUKKAH, technically not a holiday since work is not prohibited during this eight-day celebration, has achieved an unprecedented prominence in our time. Until the second half of the twentieth-century Hanukkah was of minor importance. Indeed, there had been uncertainty about Hanukkah. The Talmud, that magisterial work that had so carefully structured the Jewish holidays and pieties, asks, "What of Hanukkah?"[1] This is the only celebration about which it asks such a question. Although Purim is also not a holiday in the technical sense, an entire tractate of the Talmud is devoted to it. But Hanukkah is usually referred to only in passing.

THE MIRACLE OF A CRUSE OF OIL

Traditionally, the celebration of Ḥanukkah has been minor: the lighting of candles (or oil), one candle added each night, following the view of the Hillelites. Lighting the candles commemorates the miracle of the cruse of oil burning for eight days. And there are additions to the liturgy recited during Ḥanukkah: the hallelujah psalms and references to the divinely granted Hasmonean (Maccabean) victories. But the liturgy of these eight days does not mention the miracle of the cruse of oil.

Only the medieval spinning-top (dreidl) game has a reference to this miracle, its four letters forming the acronym for "a great miracle was there," without specifying what the miracle was. The traditional sources do not refer to the miracle as "great." It is only the dreidl, with its letters that were derived from the medieval dice of German gamblers, that proclaim the miracle as "great."[2]

THE AMERICAN CHRISTMAS CONTEXT

Ḥanukkah, beginning on the twenty-fifth day of Kislev, has become very important in recent decades, particularly in the United States, because it occurs in December. Jewish parents face the problem of the cultural, American Christmas as a temptation for their children. The Talmud's question seems to foreshadow the question that Jewish parents in America would eventually raise: "What's with Ḥanukkah? It can't hold a candle to Christmas."

STRUCTURED BY COMMERCIAL INTERESTS

The American Christmas, which has spread throughout the Western world and beyond, even as far away as non-Christian Japan, is a late nineteenth- and early twentieth-century creation by department stores. By virtue of exploitation, exaggeration, and decoration, these commercial institutions gave added importance to older motifs of pagan and Christian origin.

This American Christmas, structured by commercial interests, is remarkably rich in symbols, motifs, and activities. The Christmas tree, non-Christian in origin, is so obviously pagan that

Christians have, at times, banned its use. The yule log, holly, stockings hung at the hearth, and so much else in the American Christmas have nothing to do with the Christian savior but are remnants of pagan pieties.

Furthermore, Santa Claus is, for many an American gentile, more central to the season than the Christian savior. This jolly old man of the frozen north is full of good cheer and gifts for all. He comes in his sled pulled by reindeer, each of which has a name. Santa comes at night when all is silent and not a creature is stirring. Santa, therefore, never encounters the world of history. He comes from the uninhabited far north where there is no human history; he enters a world in which all are asleep, and sleep time is ahistoric time.

A counterpart to the old man of the frozen north is the babe in the crib (or crèche). This nativity representation, first structured by Francis of Assisi in the thirteenth century, is a barn scene of a baby in a crib surrounded by upright, adoring human figures, including three Magians, and some cattle. These figures are inert statues. None stirs. All are silent. The babe in the crib represents the Christian savior.

THE MAGIC OF ITS TIMELESSNESS

Santa Claus, the old man of the north, and the babe in the crib are the two central symbols of the American Christmas. These symbols convey a message: an old man has no future; an infant has no past. They are the incarnation of the American Christmas, which is a magic wonderland, an enchanted world above and beyond time. Santa, the old man without a future, comes from his timeless, ahistoric world into a world asleep. The crèche-scene baby, without a past, is in a barn where history does not take place. Barns are agricultural, not historical, spaces. And it is fitting that there are Magians (Matt. 2:1ff) in the nativity scene because the American Christmas is a magical, enchanted world. The magic of the American Christmas is its timelessness. That is why American gentiles dream about a white Christmas; for a white, snowbound, not-a-creature-is-stirring world is an ahistoric, mythical world.

PURITY AND POLITICS AS COORDINATES

The American Christmas is jolly, merry, plenitudinous. It is a sumptuous, dazzling celebration, assimilating to itself even such musical compositions as the *Nutcracker Suite* with its mythical theme of timelessness. Ḥanukkah, in comparison, is paltry. It does not offer much: a menorah, pancakes, a spinning-top game, and some additions to the liturgy such as references to the Hasmoneans and the victories that God granted them. Ḥanukkah is the celebration of a military victory and of a purification that took place at a particular time. On the one hand is the tradition that promotes the miracle of the cruse of oil burning for eight days. On the other hand is the tradition that emphasizes the battles and victory. They seem to be mutually exclusive.

TWO HISTORICAL THEMES

These two themes are, however, one. Both are involved with history. This is clarified by the social scientist Mary Douglas. In her *Purity and Danger*, she writes:

> The Israelites were always in their history a hard pressed minority. In their beliefs all the bodily issues were polluting . . . The threatened boundaries of their body politic would be mirrored in their care for the integrity, unity and purity of the physical body.[3]

In *Natural Symbols* Professor Douglas returns to the question of Jewish purity rules. Reflecting on 1 Maccabees 1 she comments, "Throughout the subsequent narrative of the overthrow of the invading armies and the purification of the Temple three themes are treated as coordinate symbols: defilement of the Temple, defilement of the body, breach of the law."[4] She sums up:

> The story of the Maccabees teaches that the Israelites took the purity of the Temple and the purity of the human body to represent adherence to all details of the law and so a total turning of each person in his own body and of the whole nation in the Temple and in the law toward God . . . The high walls they built around Mt. Sion and the strong guard they set upon their mouths [the reference

is to the prohibition against eating pork] were the symbolic ramparts of their commitment to their religion.[5]

The purification of the Temple, the miracle of the cruse of oil, and the military victory are interrelated. Purity and politics are coordinates. Ḥanukkah celebrates the world of history. It offers no enchantment. Jewish celebrations are celebrations of that which takes place in time, in the everyday world.

HISTORY AS INTERPRETATION

Ḥanukkah is so historically oriented that the historical serves as a principle of interpretation. Even the half-forgotten, quaint custom of eating cheese on Ḥanukkah is traditionally interpreted as the commemoration of the military victory over Holofernes made possible by Judith, who ate cheese in order to avoid non-kosher food during her stay in his tent.[6] The nineteenth-century zealous champion of Orthodoxy, Moses (Chatam) Sofer, reflecting on the Mishnah's silence about the miracle of the cruse of oil, interpreted that silence historically. Rabbi Judah, the Mishnah's redactor, consciously avoided any references to the miracle, according to Moses Sofer, because he "was of the seed of King David and the miracle of Ḥanukkah was performed through the efforts of the Hasmonean Dynasty which seized the sovereignty, although they were not Davidic. This was an evil thing for our holy master. So when he wrote the Mishnah under the influence of the Holy Spirit, [the account of] the miracle was deleted from his composition."[7] Jewish piety is so historically oriented that Jewish hermeneutics, too, embody an awareness of historical reality.

Notes

INTRODUCTION

1. Deut. 26:5-9.
2. Yi-fu Tuan, *Space and Place* (Minneapolis: University of Minnesota, 1977), 130.
3. J. Muilenberg, "The Biblical View of Time," *Harvard Theological Review* 54 (1960), 225–52.
4. Ibid.

CHAPTER 1: SABBATH: COVENANTAL TIME

1. Num. 15:32; Exod. 16:27.
2. Midrash Rabbah, Exod. 1:28.
3. Tractate *Sabbath*, 10b.
4. Ibid., 118b, Soncino translation.
5. Tractate *Bezah*, 16a.
6. Johannes Pedersen, *Israel: Its Life and Culture* (London: Oxford University, 1947), vol. 1, 296.
7. Tractate *Sanhedrin*, 38a, Tosafot.
8. Judah ben Barzillai, *Sefer ha-Ittim*, ed. R. J. Schorr (Cracow, 1902; Jerusalem, 1964, photocopy), 25.
9. Tractate *Sabbath*, 119a.
10. W. H. Hudson, *A Hind in Richmond Park* (London and Toronto: J. M. Dent, 1935), 86.
11. E. D. Starbuck, "The Intimate Senses as Sources of Wisdom," *Journal of Religion* 1, no. 2 (1923), 134.
12. Ibid., 133.
13. Hudson, op. cit., 77.
14. Ibid., 64.
15. Hans Jonas, *The Phenomenon of Life* (New York: Delta, 1966), 154.
16. Starbuck, op. cit., 134.
17. Rashi, tractates *Bezah*, 16a, and *Taanit*, 27b.
18. Midrash Rabbah, Gen. 11:8.
19. Chaim Rabin, "The Song of Songs and Tamil Poetry," *Studies in Religion* 3 (1973), 205–19.
20. Ibid., 215–16.
21. Ibid., 217.
22. Ibid.

23. Lev. 19:18; Deut. 6:5; Hos. 11:1; Jer. 31:3.
24. Pedersen, op. cit., 309.
25. Kenneth Burke, *The Rhetoric of Religion* (Berkeley and Los Angeles: University of California, 1970), 19.
26. Gaston Bachelard, *The Psychoanalysis of Fire* (Boston: Beacon, 1964), 10.
27. Ibid.
28. O. C. Stewart, "Fire as the First Great Force Employed by Man," in *Man's Role in Changing the Face of the Earth*, ed. U. L. Thomas, Jr. (Chicago: University of Chicago, 1956), 129.
29. Erich Fromm, *The Forgotten Language* (New York: Grove, 1951), 244–45.
30. Ibid., 249.
31. P. Fraisse, *The Psychology of Time*, trans. J. Leith (New York: Harper & Row, 1963), 289.
32. Pedersen, op. cit., 155, 479, 486.
33. Ibid., 481.
34. Ibid., 325.
35. Noteworthy is the fact that the *International Encyclopedia of the Social Sciences* has an article on alienation but none on intimacy.
36. *The Sociology of Georg Simmel*, trans. and ed. K. H. Wolff (New York: Free Press, 1950), 126.
37. Ibid.
38. Ibid., 127.
39. Ibid., 126.
40. Ibid.
41. Ibid., 135.
42. Ibid., 123.
43. Its source is the Zohar and it is found in the *Nusach S'fard* liturgy.
44. M. Jastrow, *A Dictionary of the Targumim, the Talmud Babli and Yerushalmi, and the Midrashic Literature* (New York, Berlin, London: Shapiro, Vallentine & Co., 1926), 961; F. Brown, S. R. Driver, and C. A. Briggs, *A Hebrew and English Lexicon of the Old Testament* (Oxford: Clarendon, 1962), 691; Pedersen, op. cit., 305.

CHAPTER 2: PASSOVER: THE SEDER AS ENTREE INTO HISTORY

1. Mircea Eliade, *Cosmos and History* (New York: Harper & Row, 1959), xi.
2. Ibid.
3. Ibid., 5.
4. 2 Chron. 30:6-8.
5. 2 Kings 23:22-23.

6. Exod. 13:14.

7. D. Karelenstein, *Maagle Tzedek, Orach Hayim* (Jerusalem: N.p., 1964–65), 102, 105.

8. Tractate *Pesahim*, 115b.

9. Erwin Straus, "Man: A Questioning Being," in *Phenomenological Psychology* (New York: Basic Books, 1966), 166, 175–76.

10. Ibid., 183.

11. Ibid., 184.

12. Ibid., 185.

13. Johannes Pedersen, *Israel: Its Life and Culture*, vol. 1, 418.

14. Ibid., 418–19.

15. Ibid., 187.

16. J. Mann, *Texts and Studies* (New York: KTAV, 1972 reprint), vol. 2, 139.

17. Sh. Yehoshua, *Pesach B'Beth El* (Holon, Israel, 1972), 8.

18. H. Schauss, *The Jewish Festivals* (Cincinnati: American Hebrew Congregations, 1938), 38.

19. *Pesach Muvin* (Livorno, 1788), 28b.

20. *Mishnah Brurah* (New York and Jerusalem, n.d.), vol. 6, 168.

21. Eliade, op. cit., 34.

22. *Mishnah Brurah*, vol. 5, 175, "BER HETEV."

23. Cf. *The Oxford Classical Dictionary* (Oxford: Clarendon, 1949), 872.

24. Michel Foucault, *The Archaeology of Knowledge* (New York: Harper & Row, 1976), 231.

25. Michel Foucault, *Mental Illness and Psychology* (New York: Harper & Row, 1976), 23.

26. Cf. S. Stern, "The Influence of Symposia Literature on the Literary Form of the Pesach Haggadah," *Journal of Jewish Studies* 8, no. 1 (1957), 13–44.

27. David Cohen, *Kol Ha-Nevuah* (Jerusalem: Mosad Ha-Rav Kook, 1970).

28. Pedersen, op. cit., vol. 1, 100.

29. Ibid.

30. *Mahzor Vitry* (Berlin, 1890), vol. 2, 304.

31. Stanley Rosen, *Plato's Symposium* (New Haven: Yale University, 1969).

32. Ibid., xix.

33. Ibid.

34. Ibid., 3.

35. Ibid., 1.

36. Ibid., 4.

37. Ibid., 5.

38. Ibid., 3.

39. Alvin Gouldner, *Enter Plato* (New York and London: Basic Books, 1965), 387.

40. *Seder Haggadah Shel Hag Ha-Pesach K'Phy-Minhag Ha-Yehudim Ha-Karaim* (Jerusalem: N.p., 1961).

41. Straus, op. cit., 169.

42. Ibid., 172.

43. Ibid., 181.

44. Ibid., 166.

45. Ibid., 187.

46. *Haggadah Shel Pesach* (Tel Aviv: United Artists Ltd., 1965), unpaginated. The translations from Hebrew to English are mine.

47. Straus, op. cit., 187.

48. Karl Lowith, *Meaning in History* (Chicago: University of Chicago, 1949), 4.

49. Ibid.

50. Ibid., 194–96.

51. Quoted in Lowith, op. cit., 17–18.

52. Ibid., 18.

53. Ernst Cassirer, *The Philosophy of Symbolic Forms*, vol. 3, *The Phenomenology of Knowledge* (New Haven: Yale University, 1957), 188.

54. Lowith, op. cit., 6.

55. G. Van Der Leeuw, *Religion in Essence and Manifestation* (New York: Harper & Row, 1968), vol. 2, 631.

56. Targum Pseudo Jonathan.

57. Tractate *Rosh HaShanah*, 11b.

58. Erwin Straus, "Awakeness," in *Phenomenological Psychology*, 115.

59. Ibid., 112.

60. Ibid., 116.

61. Erwin Straus, "The Upright Posture," in *Phenomenological Psychology*, 145.

CHAPTER 3: SHAVUOT: THE CELEBRATION OF REVELATION

1. *Midrash Lekah Tov* (Israel, n.d.), vol. 2, "Emor," 130 (my translation).

2. Ibid., "R'ay," 27.

3. Midrash Rabbah, Song of Songs, chap. 1, section 12 (Soncino translation).

4. *Magen Avraham* commentary to *Shulhan Arukh*, "Orah Hayyim," Laws of Shavuot, Section 484.

5. V. Aubert and H. White, "Sleep, A Sociological Interpretation," in *Sociology and Everyday Life*, ed. M. Truzzi (Englewood Cliffs, N.J.: Prentice-Hall, 1968), 325.

6. Ibid., 330.

7. Ibid., 335.

8. Ibid.

9. Erwin Straus, *The Primary World of the Senses* (New York: Free Press of Glencoe, 1963), 275.

10. Ibid., 278.

11. Ibid., 288.

12. Ibid., 289.

13. Ibid.

14. Ibid.

15. Ibid., 283.

16. *Pirkei de Rabbi Eliezer* (Jerusalem: N.p., 1963), 96b (my translation).

17. Midrash Rabbah, Exod. 28:6 (Soncino translation).

18. *Mekilta de Rabbi Ishmael*, ed. and trans. J. Z. Lauterbach (Philadelphia: Jewish Publication Society, 1949), vol. 2, 232–33.

19. L. Wittgenstein, *On Certainty* (New York: Harper & Row, 1972), 25.

20. *Sifrei de Bei Rav* (New York: Om Press, 1929), 79a (my translation).

21. *The Sociology of Georg Simmel*, 188.

22. As quoted by Jean Hyppolite, *Studies on Marx and Hegel* (New York: Harper & Row, 1973), 36.

23. Mircea Eliade, *The Sacred and Profane* (New York: Harper & Row, 1961), 205.

24. *Pirkei Avot* 6:6 (the translation is that of H. Danby, *The Mishnah*, Oxford: Clarendon, 1933).

25. Midrash Rabbah on Exod. 27:9 (Soncino translation).

26. Tractate *Baba Kamma*, 85b (Soncino translation).

27. David Cohen, *Kol Ha-Nevuah*.

28. Hans Jonas, *The Phenomenon of Life*, 139.

29. Ibid., 136.

30. Ibid., 137.

31. Ibid., 144.

32. Tractate *Sabbath*, 88a.

33. Michel Foucault, *The Archaeology of Knowledge*, 22–23.

34. *Pirkei Avot* 6:6 (Danby translation).

35. The phrase is Sartre's. Cf. Jean Paul Sartre, *Being and Nothingness*, trans. Hazel E. Barnes (New York: Washington Square Press, 1966), 5.

36. M. Minkowski, *Lived Time* (Evanston: Northwestern University, 1970), 101.

37. M. Gaster, *Maaseh Book* (Philadelphia: Jewish Publication Society, 1934), vol. 2, 338.

38. *Sefer Baal Shem Tov* (Jerusalem, 1974), 63–64.

39. Ibid., 127.

40. H. Gadamer, *Philosophical Hermeneutics* (Berkeley and Los Angeles: University of California, 1977), 38.

41. Ludwig Feuerbach, *The Essence of Christianity* (New York: Harper & Row, 1957), 83.

42. E. Straus, *Phenomenological Psychology*, 175–76.

43. Michel Foucault, *The Order of Things* (New York: Vintage, 1973), xix–xx. His emphasis on the visual should be noted.

44. Foucault, *The Archaeology of Knowledge*, 22–23.

45. Peter Berger, *The Sacred Canopy* (Garden City, N.Y.: Doubleday, 1967), 5.

46. Ibid., 22.

47. P. Berger and T. Luckmann, *The Social Construction of Reality* (Garden City, N.Y.: Doubleday, 1976).

48. *Sefer ha-Zohar* (Jerusalem: N.p., 1960), vol. 14, 71 (my translation).

49. Ibid., vol. 7, 216 (my translation).

50. Berger and Luckmann, op. cit., 112.

CHAPTER 4: ROSH HA-SHANAH: THE DAY OF REMEMBRANCE

1. Tractate *Rosh Ha-Shana*, 16a (Soncino translation).

2. Ibid.

3. Mircea Eliade, *Myth and Reality* (New York: Harper & Row, 1968), 120.

4. Mircea Eliade, *Cosmos and History*, 43.

5. Ibid., 44.

6. Gen. 22:12.

7. Johannes Pedersen, *Israel: Its Life and Culture*, vol. 1, 107.

8. Ernst Cassirer, *The Philosophy of Symbolic Forms*, vol. 3, 88.

9. Ibid., 180.

10. E. Minkowski, *Lived Time*, 157.

11. Cassirer, op. cit., 167.

12. Quoted by Shmuel Agnon, *Days of Awe* (English translation, New York: Schocken, 1948), 70–72.

13. H. Frankfort, *Kingship and the Gods* (Chicago: University of Chicago, 1955), 319.

14. Ibid., 314.

15. Eliade, *Cosmos and History*, 57.

16. Ibid., 81.

17. Ibid., 85.

18. Eliade, *Myth and Reality*, 62.

19. B. S. Childs, *Memory and Tradition in Israel* (Naperville, Ill.: A. R. Allenson, 1962), 34.

20. Ibid., 33.

21. Ibid., 42.
22. Ibid.
23. Ibid., 52, 58.
24. Ibid., 60.
25. Ibid.
26. E. Partridge, *Origins* (New York: Macmillan, 1958), 463, "Pain," para. 7.

CHAPTER 5: YOM KIPPUR: THE DAY OF FORGIVENESS

1. Usually translated in the singular; our use of the plural follows the Hebrew. An old tradition interprets the plural as referring to both the living and the dead.
2. Maimonides, *Mishneh Torah*, "Laws of Repentance," 1:1.
3. Erwin Straus, *Phenomenological Psychology*, 163.
4. *Shulhan Arukh*, "Orah Hayyim," Laws of Yom Ha-Kippurim, Section 607, para. 3.
5. Straus, op. cit., 139.
6. Ibid., 164.
7. *Sefer Mahril*, as quoted in the *Encyclopedia Talmudit* (Jerusalem, 1965), vol. 11, "Viduy."
8. Straus, op. cit., 146.
9. Ibid., 147.
10. C. E. Izard, ed., *Human Emotions* (New York: Plenum Press, 1977), 424.
11. *The Book of Jubilees*, ed. and trans. R. H. Charles (London: A. & C. Black, 1902), chap. 25, v. 18–19.
12. *Seder Olam Rabbah* (Jerusalem, N.p., 1965), vol. 1, chap. 6; Tractate *Baba Bathra*, 121a; Tractate *Ta'anith*, 30b.
13. Cf. *Encyclopaedia Judaica* (Jerusalem and New York: Keter, 1971), vol. 15, cols. 1006–1008.
14. Two versions of the martyrology are available in A. Jellinek's *Bet Ha-Midrash* (Jerusalem, 1938 offprint), vol. 2, 64–72, vol. 6, 19–35. The traditional prayerbook uses a shorter version.
15. Tractate *Berakoth*, 21b (Soncino translation).
16. E. W. Budge, *The Egyptian Book of the Dead* (New York: Dover, 1967 reprint), 347–49.

CHAPTER 6: SUCCOT: SPACE IN HISTORY

1. Tractate *Succah*, 11b.
2. Ibid.

3. *Mishnah Brurah Commentary to the Shulkan Aruch* (Jerusalem and New York, n.d.), vol. 6, 168–69. Quoted in the name of Jacob ben Asher, "The Tur." The translation of the passage is mine.

4. Gaston Bachelard, *The Poetics of Space* (Boston: Beacon, 1969).

5. Ibid., 31.

6. Ibid., 32.

7. Ibid.

8. Gaston Bachelard, *The Poetics of Reverie* (Boston: Beacon, 1969), 14, 100.

9. Ibid., 117, 119.

10. Ibid., 116.

11. Ibid., 111.

12. Ibid., 128.

13. Mircea Eliade, *Cosmos and History,* xi.

14. Ibid., 35.

15. C. A. Weslager, *The Delaware Indians: A History* (New Brunswick, N.J.: Rutgers University, 1972), 13.

16. F. G. Speck, *A Study of the Delaware Indian Big House Ceremony* (Harrisburg, Pa.: Pennsylvania Historical Commission, 1931), 22.

17. Weslager, op. cit., 69.

18. Ibid.

19. Speck, op. cit., 81.

20. F. G. Speck, *Oklahoma Delaware Ceremonies, Feasts and Dances* (Philadelphia: American Philosophical Society, 1937), 22.

21. Weslager, op. cit., 14.

22. *Sefer Ha-Rokeach Ha-Gadol,* ed. B. S. Sherman (Jerusalem, 1966), 117. The translation of the passage is mine.

23. Cf. Philip Goodman, *The Sukkot and Simhat Torah Anthology* (Philadelphia: Jewish Publication Society, 1973), illustration nos. 8, 10, 13.

24. Tractate *Succah,* 2b.

25. Moses Mat, *Mateh Moshe* (Warsaw, 1876, photostat), 178.

26. Cf. Goodman, op. cit., illustration no. 12, and *Encyclopaedia Judaica,* vol. 9, col. 1587, fig. 142.

27. Cf. *The Traditional Prayer Book for Sabbaths and Festivals,* ed. and trans. David De Sola Pool (Hyde Park, N.Y.: University Books, 1960), 633–36.

28. Tractate *Succah,* 20b. Rashi's first gloss to chap. 2.

29. Mordecai Ha-Cohen, *Siftey Cohen* (Jerusalem: Y. Goldman Press, 1964), vol. 2, 114. The translation of the passage is mine.

30. Both terms are used in rabbinic literature, but "succah of Sodom" is rather rare.

31. Ephraim Solomon ben Aaron of Luntshits, *Olelot Efraim* (Tel Aviv: Pardes Press, 1964), 116. The translation of the passage is mine.

32. *Pesikta d' Rab Kahana*, ed. Solomon Buber (Lyck, 1868, photo offset, New York, 1949), 189a. The translation of the passage is mine.

33. Cf. *Seder Avodat Yisrael*, ed. Y. Baer (Germany: Schocken, 1936), 382.

34. *The Writings of Maharal of Prague* (Hebrew), ed. A. Karib (Jerusalem: Mosad Ha-Rav Kook, 1960), vol. 2, 376.

CHAPTER 7: TEFILLAT GESHEM: THE JEWISH PRAYER FOR RAIN

1. M. C. Stevenson, *The Zuni Indians* (Washington: Twenty-third Annual Report of the Bureau of American Ethnology, 1904).

2. F. D. McCarthy, "Aboriginal Rain Makers and Their Ways," *The Australian Museum Magazine* 10, no. 8, 250.

3. Ibid., 251; and A. W. Howitt, *Native Tribes of South-East Australia* (London: Macmillan, 1904), 394.

4. Howitt, op. cit., 395.

5. McCarthy, op. cit., 10, no. 9, 304–5.

6. B. Spencer and F. I. Gillen, *The Northern Tribes of Central Australia* (Osterhoot, N.B., Netherlands, 1969 reprint of 1904 ed.), 314.

7. Ibid., 314–15.

8. Translation of Paltiel Birnbaum in his *Daily Prayerbook* (New York, 1949), 702, modified by me.

9. A. Buchler, *Some Types of Palestinian Piety* (Westmead, England, 1966 reprint of 1904 ed.), 246.

10. *Encyclopaedia Judaica*, vol. 8, col. 964.

11. Buchler, op. cit., 248.

12. Ibid., 246.

13. Ibid., 248.

14. Tractate *Ta'anith*, 23a.

CHAPTER 8: THE PRIESTLY BLESSING: A PRAYER CONCERNING DREAMS

1. The text of the Priestly Blessing is given in Num. 6:24-26:
The Lord bless thee and keep thee;
The Lord make His face to shine upon
thee, and be gracious unto thee;
The Lord lift up His countenance
upon thee, and give thee peace.
(JPS Bible translation, Philadelphia, 1917).

2. The translation I have used (and, at points, modified) is that of *The Daily Prayerbook, Translated and Annotated with an Introduction* by Philip Birnbaum (New York: Hebrew Publishing Co., 1949), 628–32.

3. Tractate *Berakot*, 55b.

4. Ibid.
5. 2 Kings 20; Isaiah 38; Num. 12:10-15; 2 Kings 5.
6. Exod. 15:23-25; 2 Kings 2:19-22.
7. Erwin Straus, *The Primary World of the Senses*, 278, 288.
8. A. Leo Oppenheim, *Dreams in the Ancient Near East*, American Philosophical Society Transactions, New Series, vol. 46, part 3 (Philadelphia: American Philosophical Society, 1956), 226.
9. Straus, op. cit., 278.
10. Hans Jonas, *The Phenomenon of Life*, 137.
11. Ibid., 154-58.
12. Johannes Pedersen, *Israel: Its Life and Culture*, vol. 1, 182-99.
13. Ibid., 198.
14. Ibid., 149.
15. S. J. Korchin, *Modern Clinical Psychology* (New York: Basic Books, 1976), 129.
16. Pedersen, op. cit., 304.
17. Ibid., p. 309.
18. Quoted in Korchin, op. cit., 284.

CHAPTER 9: THE NINTH OF AV: THE SORROWS OF EXILE

1. *Kinot for the Ninth of Av*, translated and annotated by the Rev. Abraham Rosenfeld (London: I. Labworth & Co., 1965), 121. All liturgical quotations are from this edition, subsequently referred to as *Kinot*, except where otherwise noted.
2. *Kinot*, 148-49.
3. Ibid., 168-70.
4. Ibid., 132-34.
5. Ibid., 93-94.
6. Ibid., 122.
7. Ibid., 111-12.
8. Ibid., 114.
9. Ibid., 144-45.
10. Y. T. Lewinski, *Sefer Ha-Moadim* (Tel Aviv: Dvir Co., 1963), vol. 7, 406-7.
11. *Kinot*, 36.
12. Lewinski, op. cit., 326-27.
13. Ibid., 405.
14. K. Lowith, *Meaning in History*, 194.
15. Ibid., 195.
16. Lamentations 3:66.
17. Erwin Straus, *Phenomenological Psychology*, 243.

18. Arthur Schopenhauer, *The World as Will and Representation* (New York: Dover, 1966), vol. 1, 376.
19. Ibid.
20. Ibid., 377.
21. Ibid.
22. Ibid.
23. Ibid.
24. Esther 2:6 and 4:1.

CHAPTER 10: PURIM: THE CELEBRATION OF DISORDER

1. Tractate *Megillah*, 13a; *Yalkut Shimoni*, "Esther," 1053.
2. Esther 3:6.
3. Esther 3:8.
4. Esther 2:6.
5. Jeremiah 29:7.
6. Esther 1:17, 20, 22.
7. Tractate *Megillah*, 15b. This is usually translated as "fickle-minded."
8. A. I. Sperling, *Taamey Ha-Minhagim* (Jerusalem: Eshkol, 1957), 376.
9. Esther 8:17.
10. Esther 8:15.
11. *Ohev Israel* (Jerusalem, 1966), 111.
12. Quoted in Jacques Ehrmann, "Homo Ludens Revisited," in *Game, Play, Literature*, ed. Jacques Ehrmann (Boston: Beacon, 1971), 37.
13. Eric Voegelin, "Order and History," vol. 1, *Israel and Revelation* (Baton Rouge: Louisiana State University Press, 1956), 165–66.
14. J. Wistinetzki and J. Freiman, *Sefer Hasidim* (Berlin: 1924), para. 703.
15. Erwin Straus, *The Primary World of the Senses*, 326.
16. Tractate *Megillah*, 7b.
17. For a summary of the legal material, cf. J. D. Epstein, *Otzar Haiggeret* (New York: Torat Ha-adam, 1968), 104–6.
18. 1 Sam. 15:9.
19. Cf. R. Alcalay, *Words of the Wise* (Jerusalem: Massada, 1970), 395.
20. Quoted by Eugen Fink in "The Oasis of Happiness: Toward an Ontology of Play," translated from the German and abridged by U. & T. Saine in *Game, Play, Literature*.
21. Ibid., 23.
22. Kenneth Burke, *Attitudes Toward History*, vol. 1 (New York: New Republic, 1937), 220.
23. Ibid., 224.
24. James Faris, *Cat Harbour: A Newfoundland Fishing Settlement* (St. John's, Newfoundland: Newfoundland Social and Economic Studies No. 3, 1966).

25. Ibid., 194.
26. Ibid., 200.
27. Ibid., 204. Weddings are distinguished from marriages, the latter being the religious service.
28. Ibid., 206.
29. Ibid., 207.
30. E. Partridge, *Origins*, 528.
31. Cf. Isaiah Hurwitz, *The Two Tablets of the Covenant* (Tel Aviv, 1959), vol. 2, 48 (Hebrew).
32. Faris, op. cit., 210.
33. Ibid., 211.
34. Cf. Y. T. Lewinski, *Sefer Ha-Moadim*, vol. 6, 30, for the sources.
35. *Midrash Talpiot* (Czernowitz, 1860), 141.

CHAPTER 11: HANUKKAH: PURITY AND POLITICS IN HISTORY

1. Tractate *Sabbath*, 21b.
2. *Encyclopaedia Judaica*, vol. 6, col. 1393.
3. Mary Douglas, *Purity and Danger* (London: Penguin, 1966), 48.
4. Mary Douglas, *Natural Symbols* (New York: Vintage, 1973), 61.
5. Ibid., 64.
6. Abraham Danzig, *Hayye Adam* (Wilna, 1925), Rule 154, para. 3.
7. Quoted in A. I. Sperling, *Taamey Ha-Minhagim*, "Matters of Hanukkah," para. 847 (my translation).

Glossary

AFIKOMAN

The last piece of matzah that one is obligated to eat at the Passover Seder.

AGGADAH

Aggadah means narration and connotes all in the Talmud that is not of a legal nature: stories, homilies, legends, maxims. *Aggadic* describes something from the aggadah.

AHAD HA-AM

The pen name of Asher Ginzberg (1856–1927), essayist and social critic. The pseudonym means "one of the people."

BAAL SHEM TOV

Master of the Good Name, title given to Israel ben Eliezer (c. 1700–1760), founder of Hasidism.

BET MIDRASH

House of study. A hall where advanced Talmud students gather for study, discussion, and prayer.

ELOHIM

A term for God.

ERETZ YISRAEL

The Land of Israel.

GEMARA

The multivolume commentary and extension-development of the Mishnah; popular term for the Talmud, which includes both the Mishnah and Gemara.

HAGGADAH

The Passover liturgical text recited at the Seder. *Haggadot* is the plural form.

HALAKIST

From *halakah*, which means "way" and connotes "law." A halakist is an interpreter of Jewish law.

121

HAMANTASCHEN	Three-cornered pieces of pastry eaten on Purim.
HAMETZ	Leavened products, whose usage is prohibited on Passover.
HA-SHOMER HA-TZAIR HAGGADAH	Secular Zionist Passover liturgical text produced in the state of Israel.
HILLELITES	Followers of the hermeneutic tradition of Hillel (first century C.E.), one of the most important sages in the Mishnah.
HOSHANNAH RABBAH	Popular name for the seventh day of the Succot festival.
KABBALISTS	Traditional Jewish mystics.
KARAITES	A Jewish community that rejects rabbinic Judaism; originated in the eighth century C.E. A sizable Karaite group lives in Israel.
KARPAS	The vegetable dipped in salt water and eaten at the Seder in order to taste the bitterness of slavery.
KIDDUSH	Sanctification. Blessings recited over the wine at the commencement of the Seder or over the wine or bread at Sabbath and other holy meals.
L'CHA DODI	"Come My Beloved," a hymn welcoming Queen Sabbath, composed by Solomon Alkabetz in the sixteenth century, sung in the synagogue during the Friday service at sunset.
MATTAN TORAH	[God's] giving the Torah.

MATZAH	The unleavened bread eaten at the Seder and during the entire Passover festival.
MIDRASH	Collections of rabbinic interpretations of Scripture.
MISHNAH	A collection of rabbinic law redacted by Rabbi Judah ha-Nasi, c. 200 C.E., in Sepphoris, Galilee.
MITZVOT	Commandments [given by God]. Traditional Jewish pieties and practices: prayers, dietary rules, festivals, and social and economic regulations. The singular form is *mitzvah*.
NESHAMAH YETERAH	Usually translated "additional soul." A better translation-explanation is given by Rashi (1040–1105 C.E.): "A greater amplitude for food and drink."
OMER, COUNTING OF	The forty-nine days counted from the day that the first sheaf of newly harvested barley was offered in the ancient Jerusalem Temple, with the fiftieth day being Shavuot, the Festival of Weeks, which celebrates God's giving the Torah.
PESACH DOROT	The Passover celebration of all subsequent generations after the Exodus from Egypt.
PESACH MIZRAIM	The first Passover supper celebrated before the departure from Egypt.
PESACH SHENI	The Passover celebrated in ancient Temple times by those who, because of their impurity or distance, missed the previous month's observance of the Passover.

PURIM

The festival commemorating the victory over Haman. The word *purim* means lots, referring to the lottery cast by Haman to determine the day on which the Jews would be exterminated.

RASHA

The wicked son of the Passover Haggadah.

RASHI

The acronym for Solomon son of Isaac (1040–1105 C.E.), one of the great medieval commentators on Scripture and Talmud.

SAMARITAN
HIGH PRIEST

The Samaritans are a mixture of peoples who adopted Jewish life sometime after 721 B.C.E. Their scripture consists of the Pentateuch in the old Canaanite script. Their high priest offers a paschal lamb sacrifice on Mount Gerizim near Nablus. In contemporary Israel, they are considered an independent religious community.

SEDER

The liturgical Passover meal. *Sedarim* is the plural.

SHALOM

Peace.

SHAMMAI AND
HILLEL

Two of the most important rabbinic sages (first century B.C.E), usually in opposition in their interpretations of law. In most cases Hillel's views became the norm.

SHAVUOT

The Feast of Weeks celebrating the giving of the Torah. (*See* Omer, Counting of.)

SHOFAR

The ram's horn sounded a number of times during the morning service in the synagogue on Rosh Ha-Shanah, the New Year festival.

SHULHAN ARUKH — To date, the last comprehensive code of Jewish law, composed in the sixteenth century by Joseph Caro, jurist and mystic, in Safed.

SUCCAH — The booth in which one dwells on Succot, the holiday of Tabernacles. *Succot* is the plural form.

TALMUD — The compilation of the Mishnah and Gemara, the central work of traditional Judaism.

TARGUM — Aramaic translation-commentary to the Hebrew Scriptures.

TISHAH B'AV — The ninth day of the month of Av (July-August), which commemorates the destruction of the two ancient Jerusalem Temples, the Spanish expulsion of the Jews (1492), and other calamities.

TOLDOT — Generations. The biblical term for historical reality.

TORAH — Instruction, which can refer to the Pentateuch, the rest of Hebrew Scripture, the oral tradition (i.e., Talmud), or to all of traditional Jewish teaching and piety.

YESHIVAH — The traditional school, beyond the primary level, devoted to the study of Talmud and the rest of rabbinic literature.

YIZKOR — Memorial prayer for the dead. This rubric word of the prayer means "may He [God] remember."

ZOHAR   The major work of Jewish mysticism. It is
                         a mystical commentary to the Pentateuch
                         and other sections of Hebrew Scripture.

Subject Index